S0-FQW-069

Contents

Dedication

With immense gratitude, deep Love and humility, I offer my story to our Beloved Spiritual guide, Sri Sathya Sai Baba, in celebration of his 85th birthday.

Acknowledgements

I sincerely thank my companion Maurice, who edited and was able to help me structure my recollection of memories into a coherent form, John Behner, our Sai mentor in India and Central America, and all our dear Sai friends who encouraged me to share my lifetime experiences with our magnificent guru Sri Sathya Sai Baba, especially Phil Gosselin, Bill Harvey, and Ronne Marantz.

Introduction

For the past 40 years I have been blessed to have had interaction with Sathya Sai Baba who is a Divine Reincarnation. A year ago I underwent neurosurgery. Baba has given me an extension on planet earth. Our Sai family had me in their prayers and asked me to share my traumatic experience. So I did. Since then, many people have told me I should share my direct experiences of 40 years with the Avatar. I will try to depict the circumstances and settings and do my best to remember times and places and share my story in a simple but very sincere and loving way. Sai devotees will know exactly what I am talking about. Others may think that I lost my bearings, just as my own family did when I revealed that I had met a being whom to me is Jesus walking this earth. Who is Sathya Sai Baba? Let me introduce to you the most extraordinary being walking this earth, as directly experienced in my own life.

PREPARATION

A Young Child – Who Am I?

I am one year old, my father had the age of Christ, 33 years old when he died, leaving my mother a widow at 22. This was the typical couple depicted in telenovela plots - young beautiful woman from a lower socio-economic status marries a man from upper socio-economic status. My mother had come from Maraita, a small town in Honduras. She was an aspiring fashion designer. My father's family came from San Juancito and Valle de Angeles, mining towns. He was a real character - spoke foreign languages, worked with the Americans at the Rosario Mining Company, and was a musician. He was politically savvy; his best friend became president of the country. His caustic sense of humor was such that even 65 years after his death people still remember his jokes.

After his death my mother and I spent time in Tegucigalpa and with her family in Maraita. My grandparents, three uncles and two aunts gave me all the love I needed. The men in the family were musicians. The women cooked delicious food and baked all types of bread. At night we would sit around a fire under the moon and the stars telling stories.

My grandfather gave me a white horse. I was three and half. I put my head on a wooden fence and observed that beautiful animal. All of a sudden I said to myself: "I am Rosa, this is my horse." Is this when the sense of identity begins, when something belongs to us? Yes! I am this person, this is mine. I have my own identity.

Valle de Angeles / the Catholic Church as my playground.

When I was four years old I lived for a year in a beautiful little town in Honduras which is called Valley of the Angeles. We lived in the center of the town in a big house with a big garden, but we also spent quite a bit of time in another property up in the mountains called "La Soledad de Maria" (Mary's Solitude).

It was at this time that a young child, Maurice, my life-long soul mate, appears in my life; he was one year older than me, and had been brought to Honduras for a year, becoming my playmate and protector. We were shown a painting of two children walking in nature with an angel hovering above, our guardian angel.

A year later, I was an only child but I managed to make friends with all the children from nearby houses. We cut coffee grains; we enjoyed all kinds of fruit trees - nances, plums, guavas - we loved playing among the huge pine trees. I was probably bored at times and became mischievous. Once I saw all these baby pine trees, so I cut them and brought them to show my aunt. She was livid; the gardener had spent three days planting those trees.

I loved playing in a natural setting. We did a lot of horseback riding. I loved my horse, he was very gentle, but one day I fell and he stepped on my stomach by accident. My abdomen was purple for a few days and doctors kept a close watch on me. I was so worried for my horse. What if I died? Then my horse would most likely be severely punished. After all it was just an accident, no hard feelings. We had picnics in the countryside, we also went to the river to swim; the water was crystal clear; I loved jumping from rock to rock. The property smelled of jasmine; there were all types of flowers, plants and huge trees.

Years later in New York, I took a phonetics workshop with Doe Lang, an actress who had written a book *Charismedia*. The first exercise was to lie down on the floor, relax and try to remember our very first memory. My mind went to that incredibly beautiful setting where one Sunday right after mass, I was wearing my Sunday best, which was a white taffeta with lace dress, and black patent shoes. I took off my shoes and walked in the mud along the lilies; the fragrance was what I liked. Doe Lang thought I had the most beautiful first memory. Yes! I was one with nature.

My uncle got me toys that were really neat. I had the best collection of soldiers from England. My aunt distracted herself by teaching me how to read when I was four and a half. I memorized a whole book but she thought I was really reading; she would show off by having me read in front of her friends.

Valle de Angeles was the closest town to San Juancito which to this day is a pristine place at the foothills of La Tigra, a rainforest. San Juancito was a mining town where the Rosario Resources company extracted gold for almost a century. My grandfather had come as a mining engineer from Ecole des Mines in Paris via Martinique. My grandmother, Honduran of Spanish descent, was a literary person who read Shakespeare, Cervantes, and so forth. Her brother had been sent to England to study medicine. Women at that time did not attend university, much less use their civic rights. Honduran women did not attain the right to vote until 1954. They were educated to be housewives. My grandmother, nonetheless, read all the medical books her brother had. Since there were no medical facilities in that remote mining town, even though miners would often suffer tremendous accidents, my grandmother became an empirical, self-taught doctor, and out of need and desire to relieve human suffering, performed surgeries. She never charged money to her patients; they would offer whatever they could - usually fruits, vegetables, etc. - after all she had to feed a dozen kids. She was a very strong woman, had six children of her own with two or three husbands and adopted another six.

My grandfather surveyed and mapped the town of Valle de Angeles. The document is written in gothic handwriting. I remember that my great aunts had trunks with gold ingots. When they ran out of money they would go to Tegucigalpa to convert the ingots for lempiras. That was their survival kit.

The local Catholic Church was my playground; my aunt, Salvadora de Lozano, was the one who decorated it, using the most beautiful flowers - lilies, roses, jasmine, you name it - she also dressed the saints, changing their robes for the different occasions - if it was Christmas in white, if it was Easter in purple. While my aunt worked, I ran all over the church; I played with marbles, but I still had to recite the rosary for hours; I went up to the tower where they had the bell. This bell was to ring a few times a day keeping the time; it rang when someone in the town passed away. Announcing death and following up with the rituals till burial was fascinating to me. Where do people go when they die?

It is in this setting that I learned about Jesus and many saints - Mary, La Dolorosa, La Medalla Milagrosa, la virgin de Guadalupe, la virgin de Suyapa (Honduran patron saint) and of course, Santa Rosa de Lima, whom I was named after. The church had beautiful sculptures and paintings, so did my aunt at her house. One of the most impressive paintings was the one with angels in heaven in the upper part and people in purgatory in the lower part. This one really scared me because I could not conceive why would anyone go to purgatory? I challenged the priests with my typical question: where do we go when we die? My father had died and I didn't understand why he had not resurrected, if Jesus had. Well, according to me, my father could walk in at any time! He too could be resurrected. I fantasized that he might be back any day and take me to do some sightseeing in heaven. The church was really a beautiful place, but I was frustrated with the priests who did not give satisfactory answers to my questions. Where is my father? What happens to people when they die? I was hoping my father would be in heaven with the angels and not in purgatory but no one could reassure me.

The priests, even the archbishop, would eat at our house. The conversations always turned to godly issues. My aunt managed to set up a dining table with starched white tablecloths, Limoges plates and Baccarat glasses. I still wonder how such precious things travelled from Europe to a remote town in Honduras. Cleanliness was paramount. We all had silverware with our own initials. In that mining area, tuberculosis was common, and in our house everything was sterilized to prevent contamination. At that time there were no antibiotics and my father as well as his younger sister had succumbed to this deadly disease.

One day I hear a lot of commotion; soon I figure out that my great-aunt Tia Catana had just died. I was the only child at the wake, but I had the guts to ask to see the casket to give the final kiss and send her to the other world.

Later on, we moved to Tegucigalpa and lived in the Episcopal Palace where the Bishop and other priests lived. This was a huge place, it was perfect for kids to run all over and play hide and seek.

My aunt, very religious and humanitarian, was very service oriented. She belonged to many organizations that would help the poor. On Fridays she organized and managed a few women who did a lot of cooking - free lunch for the poor children - everything was homemade, bread, jams, even chocolates. My aunt's kitchen was like the one depicted in the Mexican film *Water for Chocolate.* Fridays were festive; I joined the group of children and we had a ball.

Talking to People on the Other Side

My curiosity about life after death was so intense that when I was 12 years old I heard about a medium (someone that communicates with those in the spirit world). I convinced a friend of my mother's to bring me along. I really wanted to talk to my father. So, we went to a humble home. The medium asked my father's name and my name. She lit up a candle, closed her eyes, started breathing heavily and, soon enough, I heard that my father's spirit had entered her body. I asked him how he was and he said that everything was fine on the other side. He advised me to continue to be a good person and a good student. God is on your side, he said. I was so nervous - I felt I was pushing too far, no matter what I did I could never bring him back, but communication seemed possible. My mother was furious when I told her about that experience; she thought it was dangerous for my own sanity.

A couple of years later, when I was 14 years old, my pursuit of the question - "Where do we go when we die? – continued. I came across a magazine advertising Rosicrucian studies. I subscribed to receive monographs from San Jose, California. It is through this study that I first learned about reincarnation. I found these teachings very instructive but I had no privacy to practice the exercises they required. My great aunt "Goyita" was my Rosicrucian role model. She was a peaceful person with a lot of insight about life, and fiercely independent – well into her nineties, she could travel to other countries by herself, swim far into the sea, and happily danced with the younger generation.

Miracles are very much a part of Catholicism. Still a teenager, I went to La Antigua, Guatemala to pray to San Pedro de Betancourt, who had just been canonized by the Vatican. He was from the Canary Islands; a voice told him to go to Guatemala, so he did. Upon arrival, he bent over to kiss the ground and the earth shook! When I arrived I did also kiss the ground, but the earth did not even blink. Regardless, I could not but be impressed by the deep faith of his followers.

Hello New York / Bonjour Paris / Peace and Love

Growing up in Honduras, I only knew people by name, unaware of discrimination by race or religion. This was revealed to me for the first time when I came to the USA and encountered the civil rights movement. It just happened that I was invited to come on vacation to New York. I went to the American consulate and requested a resident visa. I got it!

Even after years of exposure to American films, upon arrival, I was stunned by the scale of construction and technology. Electric stairways – 'escalators' – were my first challenge at Miami airport. Television had not yet arrived to Honduras. Naturally I was glued every night to the tube with the excuse that I was learning English. I did not go to church too often but I was open-minded enough to attend synagogue on special occasions with my new Jewish friends.

I went back to Honduras but decided that Europe, especially France would be the doorway to broaden my outlook. Could Western Philosophy help me find answers? In the sixties French Existentialism was all the rage. While going to the Sorbonne in Paris, I had the opportunity to meet Jean Paul Sartre and Simone de Beauvoir. The highlight of philosophical confrontation with Jean Paul Sartre is that he would make fun of me because when a tray full of French cheeses with different shapes was passed to me, I did not know how to cut them properly. He would say: "How long have you been in France and you still don't know how to cut cheese?" My answer to him was "I bet you would not know how to eat tortillas either." All in all, I was fortunate to have been exposed to French intelligentsia. I was in awe of French culture. I felt at home. At last I was in a country where they knew how to spell my last name. But neither existentialism nor Western philosophy gave me answers that would appease my spirit.

The American dream still beckoned. American youth were bringing about a profound cultural change that included the civil rights and anti-war movements. The hippie slogan of 'love and peace' reflected a deep spiritual longing, but unfortunately created a 'generation gap' of youth in rebellion. Seeking a more structured and guided setting with ancient cultural roots, Maurice, his mother and I made a pilgrimage to Huatla, in Mexico, where the secret of mind-altering mushrooms had first been revealed to the West. This initiation acknowledged us as a family unit with a common spiritual bond. This was my birthday gift. I was grateful for a glimpse of another dimension, but my spiritual longing was only intensified. Well, coincidence after coincidence would lead the way.

Stumbling with yoga

I used to take jazz and modern dance classes near Carnegie Hall in New York. One day I pressed the wrong floor in the elevator, got out and opened the door which I expected to be my dance studio. Instead, I found a group of people standing on their heads. I had never seen a yoga asana. I was challenged and switched from dance to yoga.

An Accident kills the Car but not Me

The summer of 1969 during weekends we would go up to Napanoch, NY, two hours away from the city, to a private property converted into an artists' colony. One of those weekends in September, driving Maurice's Volkswagen camper from the mountain top down to the houses, I decided to take a shortcut and make a right turn, which turned out to be a very wrong turn. It was dark and the grass was high. I did not see a huge rock and crashed into it. I lost control of the car. I reacted very quickly, abandoned the wheel and held myself from the passenger's door. I immediately realized that if I stayed in the driver's seat I would smash my head. A deep sound came from the depth of my being.

"Oh God!" Yes, I was calling on God. I felt so hot, so nervous; I had no idea if I was badly hurt. Miraculously, I opened the roof of the van and crawled out. I touched my body thinking that I was bleeding. God had saved me – just some bruises. Suddenly, I remembered that cars can go on fire and if that were to occur the houses in the property would be endangered. I crawled back into the car and turned it off. The car was shaking; actually it was the last bit of life of the camper. The car was totaled and thrown out. The rock was baptized as Rosa's rock.

I ran to the nearest house where our friends were having dinner and I had such a nervous laugh, but I was able to tell them that I had just turned over the yellow bus. They had heard some noise but thought it was the dogs playing with garbage cans. They checked my body and realized I just had swelling in the right thigh.

Right after this mishap, on the way back to Manhattan, I was very quiet. I realized I could have been badly injured or even dead. How could I be so frivolous! All I did was work, taking evening courses at Columbia university, and go to a lot of parties; I had not set foot in a church in years.

The day after the accident I went back to work as if nothing had happened, but this was a turning point in my life. Was I going to learn more about yoga and meditation? Was I now going to seriously look into the purpose of life? Find my spiritual inclination? I went to Weiser's bookstore which carried esoteric books. I got a few and started reading *Autobiography of a Yogi* by Yogananda.

Russia or India?

I had left Honduras in 1959 at the onset of the Cuban revolution. I was wondering if the Five Year plan of Russia would give solutions to solve the poverty of Honduras and other developing countries. This sparked my interest to learn Russian and one day visit Russia. In doing research about minority groups in Russia, I made contact with the Russian Mission to the United Nations. I was given an appointment and to my amazement, a gentleman had come from Washington, DC.

He had several books for me and proceeded to tell me that in Russia there were no minority groups, but what impressed me was how knowledgeable he was about the geography, history and culture of Honduras, in contrast to most Europeans and Americans who thought Honduras was an island, or a country in Africa. I was even offered a scholarship, but I did not want to jeopardize my American residence. With much chagrin I could not take the scholarship, but I could at least visit Russia.

Now, in the fall of 1969 I find myself reading non-stop about India. I was planning to go on vacation and was still aiming to fulfill my dream of visiting Russia. My friend Chantal said to me: "All you do is read about India, why don't you go to India instead of Russia?" She made me realize that if I was so fascinated by India, why not go to India? I thought India was too remote culturally, the misery was one of the worst in the world, there were terrible diseases, plus it was too expensive to go there. I was intimidated. I was not ready to face India, but I listened to Chantal and proceeded to call Air India for airfares, anyway. I was told that in two weeks they were having a promotion for 400 dollars round trip New York/Bombay. I had no time to think, I just said: "Book me immediately".

India had become my obsession. I woke up in the morning and thought: How many days do I have left before going to that mysterious land? As part of the preparation, I made a list of holy places as best I could. As a student of the Integral Yoga Institute, I met Swami Satchidananda, who was very sweet and wise. He advised me to go to Rishikesh, to the Sivananda ashram in the Himalayas. He also pointed out Benares and other holy sites.

ENCOUNTER

Bewildered in India

It was hard for me to believe that I was on my way to India all by myself. I boarded Air India and I was in a different world - the music, the gentility of flight attendants with their beautiful saris.

I was entering a whole new world. It was so exciting. I was seeking and deep in my heart I knew I was going to meet the most incredible spiritual teachers.

Indian hospitality is more than generous; in their culture, guests are sent by the gods. At that time, I was working as a research associate in New York medical College. In the cafeteria I would meet doctors from India; I would grab them and tell them I was going to India, that I had no luggage because I was going to buy beautiful saris and dress like Indian women, so they could send gifts to their family - besides I wanted to stay with Indian families to get to know the culture. Could they help? They were gracious: by the time I got to Bombay I had a family, the Datwanis, waiting for me at the airport garland in hand. They took me home and asked me the classic question I was to hear over and over "what is your mission in India?" My mission was to connect with spiritual teachers.

My hairdresser, who was also a spiritual aspirant, told me about Indra Devi, who helped introduce yoga to the West - movie stars flocked to her beautiful place in Baja California; through her I learnt about an astrological reading called the book of Brigu.

I asked the family to call the pundit who reads the book of Brigu, to give me an appointment as soon as possible. The answer was: "Oh it takes months!" I replied "I come from Honduras in Latin America, it is very far and I don't think I will ever have the opportunity to come to India again." Miraculously, I got the appointment for the book of Brigu reading four hours after I had set foot in Bombay. Exactly at noon, the pundit took me to the roof of the building and measured my shadow. He took down my date and place of birth; we proceeded to the studio, where with a ruler, a compass, and drawing paper, he drew some triangles and performed mathematical equations. Then he got a hold of a huge book, very old, and told me "We're all in that book." The first thing he said to me was: "you lost your father when you were one year old." Bam! How could he know such an important event in my life? "Your mother is like this…" He mentioned other influential people in my life, my aunt, and said that my friendship with Maurice was karmic, we shared lives in the past; and to my surprise he said: "You will be coming to India many, many times in this lifetime." I said: "No, no need, once is enough!" Then he explained: "In your last life you lived with swamis and yogis, and in this lifetime you will find your spiritual teacher in the easiest possible way." He mentioned that I had lived in England as a writer, in the Southern part of France as a philosopher and healer, and in Peru as an Inca princess. I was stunned with the reading; I was eager to hear about the spiritual teacher, but he did not give any other hint. I didn't know what to make of this, but I was more than impressed. How did he know my father died when I was one year old?

Of course, my fantasy of the Orient presented contrasts. Although Honduras is a poor country, the poverty of Bombay seemed much worse than in Central America - the immense poverty, the beggars, the foul smells due to the unsanitary conditions at that time. But I was resolved to plunge into this culture.

I recruited one of the young women of the family I was staying with to go shopping for *saris* (traditional Indian female garment), *Punjabis* (pajama style outfit), *bindis* (forehead decoration), and Indian jewelry; she showed me how to wrap 8 yards of material around my body – a *sari* - this was the most elegant outfit I had ever had. I even got a Muslim outfit. I was going to adapt and look like women in this country but I also wanted to have a bit of fun.

Honduras' rich archeology of Mayan culture gave room for childhood fantasies, but my fascination for the East was based on books and film. As a child I read over and over *1001 Nights*. I had seen a film - *Midnight in Istanbul* - and thought: "One day I will go there and it is close to India, the land Columbus was seeking."

To indulge my fantasy, I asked to go to an evening of Indian music and dance. We ended up at the Taj Mahal Hotel discotheque, with young Indian rock and roll players. I said: "No, that's not what I want. I want an evening of enchantment with genuine Indian music and beautiful dance." We ended up at a place where women dance and sing for men, every other sentence approaching the men with folded hands in prayer pose. The men place bills on the performer's head.

My sense of adventure got the best of me. I was wearing a long chiffon dress and decided to help these entertainers make more rupees. I started dancing and collecting, passing on the bundle of rupees to the beautiful dancers: they told me that I looked like Mirabai, an Indian female saint. Only in India would I be seen as a saint! Among the men was a filmmaker, he offered to have me act in one of his films; I declined and told him that my journey to India is strictly for spiritual search. In hindsight, I missed that opportunity. Little did I know that India is the biggest producer of films in the world.

I was very impressed that even businessmen would pray before starting the business day. They pray with a lot of fervor; they have their *puja* (little prayer room) right in their office; the incense smell, the flowers and the candles were hypnotic. There were other little rituals or forms of behavior at home that called my attention. For instance: the daughter-in-law would do *padnamaskar*, bend over every morning and touch her mother-in-law's feet, requesting her blessings. Another example of gentility: a young mother would wake up an eight-year-old son by giving him a massage and singing in a whispering tone a melodious spiritual song. I thought to myself: "How beautiful!" In the West it is: "Come on, get up, get dressed, hurry up, hurry up, must rush to go to school." What a contrast! This particular family was incredible, the mother was illiterate but she controlled an empire. Her seven sons were businessmen in the USA, England, Germany, France, Italy and other countries in the Middle East. This lady spent her days sitting in a *jhoola* (hammock), talking long-distance with her sons; they all requested her advice and blessings on a daily basis. She was not a literate person, she was not an educated person, but she was a spiritual person and knew how to advise her sons when it came to the business world.

I was still in Bombay as a tourist, in awe of the museums, the temples, the Ajanta caves, but above all I wanted to get to know these beautiful polite and gentle people. I loved the food; whenever I was invited to an Indian home they were very flattered that I would love their food and I would even ask for seconds. Somehow, I felt peaceful and happy discovering something new every day.

I was invited to a wedding at the Taj Mahal Hotel. I had never seen such extravagance. The bride had jewelry everywhere: in her nose, her forehead, her hair, her necklace; bangles on the upper and lower arms, ankles, rings on her toes, her hands were painted with henna. This was the fantasy world I expected to see in India. I loved every bit of it. The musicians played non-stop. The abundance of food was impressive.

Two days before leaving for India, a friend who is an accomplished artist and lives in nature upstate New York called to tell me that he had heard of two 'groovy' (interesting) places in India. One was Goa, and the other Puttaparthi. I took notice and jotted it down in my agenda. I kept asking everybody and everywhere if they knew a place called Puttaparthi; not even the post office in Bombay knew at that time where Puttaparthi was.

In the meantime, I was invited to Poona to go to an ashram where Vaswani was the guru. I was like a museum curio there, my mere appearance aroused people's curiosity, for they had never seen a Latin American. I could feel those piercing black eyes staring at me and I wondered if they would read my soul. I was asked to stay indefinitely, I could become a landowner; but I wanted to go to Pondicherry and the Himalayas, and this place Puttaparthi was always in the back of my mind because my artist friend had recommended it very highly, even though he didn't even know what or where it was.

Utopian Society

While I was in New York, trying to get more and more information about India I had learned that the Ford Foundation was involved with a very special project in Pondicherry, a former French colony; they were building a utopian society where the energies of East and West would unite. I decided this would be an ideal experience. Auroville is a universal city, dedicated to human unity, inspired by the vision of Sri Aurobindo and the Mother, who was French, and the sole spiritual leader of the ashram since Aurobindo left his body in 1950. Since I have a French last name and I had been a student in France, I was intrigued and inspired by the mother's story.

I decided to go to Madras and contacted the Futnani family; they were most polite and had the same question for me "What is your mission in India?" I said: "My mission is to meet the French mother in Pondicherry and then go to the Himalayas." Mrs. Futnani immediately called a friend, Mr. Gupta, who often visited the Aurobindo ashram. Mr. Gupta was very impressed and praised me for my knowledge of spiritual places and teachers. I had an ardent desire to know more about the ancient wisdom of this mysterious country. Mr. Gupta proceeded to write a letter of recommendation so that I would be well received in Aurobindo's ashram and get the French Mother's *darshan*.

When Mr. Gupta was about to leave I said to him: "Thank you so much! I will be back in 10 days and I will let you know about my sojourn in Pondicherry." He responded "I will not be able to see you again because I just retired and I'm going to see my guru for a month in Puttaparthi." I jumped off my seat and in disbelief I asked him: "Puttaparthi? I have been trying to find out about that place, a very interesting person in New York told me to check it out because it is supposed to be fascinating." Mr. Gupta thought for a fraction of a minute and extended an invitation. He said to me: "I am taking my family along with me. We are taking two cars with two drivers who speak various languages, and we have room for one more person; if you get up at 4 a.m. you can come with us." I did not hesitate, I said: "I am free like a bird and I am coming with you and will postpone my trip to Pondicherry."

The next day, mid-November 1969, we left Madras at dawn, drove miles and miles stopping several times a day for personal needs, food, tea. I thought we were going to the end of the world, the roads were unpaved, lots of dust. Rural people carrying baskets of food and wood on their heads, and women often added the heavy load of a child. There were no more road signs and I started getting worried. I was wondering, "Where are these people taking me?" Finally we arrived in Puttaparthi a bit after 9 p.m. ; the ashram had just closed and we were directed to find rooms in the most squalid town I had ever seen. I was completely unprepared, after all in Bombay and Madras I had seen plush hotels and my security blanket was my American Express credit card, which was useless in such a place.

My third eye bump

I was given a room in Puttaparthi town that was totally empty. Empty, pure concrete, that was it! There was not a table, there was not a chair, much less a mattress or even a simple mat. There was nothing! I had to sleep on the concrete with my Burberry raincoat on. At 3:30 a.m. I was told to get up to go to the 4 a.m. *Omkar* (singing around the ashram). As I woke up that morning I felt something weird on my face, I had an inflammation, a bump like a tennis ball on my third eye, God knows what kind of insect bit me while I slept. I was fearful; I followed Mr. Gupta and his family to the ashram but I stayed close to Mr. Gupta for he was the only one who spoke English. Later in the morning we went for breakfast and he ordered *dosa* for me. Little did I know that I was to eat *dosa* for breakfast, lunch, and dinner for my entire stay because that was the only thing I could order, it sounded like my name Rosa.

First sight of the Avatar

Sai Baba appeared in the balcony of the *mandir*. Later on he walked around the people that were there to receive *darshan*. Ninety-nine percent were Indians who spoke Tamil, Telegu, Hindi, and some other Indian languages very strange to my ear. I was the most skeptical visitor. The amazing thing is that whenever I went to eat in the town, I wanted to pay and I would be told "it's been taken care of, no need for you to pay."

I was intrigued by this character dressed in an impeccable orange silk robe with an afro and who looked like a jazz musician. For the next three days it was drizzling. On my third day waiting for Baba to give *darshan*, a woman's *seva dal* came over and grabbed me, she was horrified that I was seated with the men. I still had my blue jeans, my raincoat and my hair was very short - no one had noticed I was a woman sitting with the men. She told me to sit with the women. At that time I was unaware of any such

37

rules.

At that point, Mr. Gupta found Sita, an Indian young woman who lived in North Africa and spoke French. She was to guide me and help me adapt to the precarious conditions of Puttaparthi. I thought she was a real fanatic. She kept telling me that Sai Baba was God. I immediately rejected such notion. As a Catholic I had seen beautiful churches in the most poor towns in Latin America, cathedrals and churches in the US and Europe. I had even been to the Vatican. The House of God for Catholics is extraordinarily beautiful, clean, well decorated, displaying the most beautiful flower arrangements. I could not conceive that God in India would choose a squalid, miserable town with lepers, people with physical deformities, destined in this life to beg for a morsel of food. I considered this to be a very unsanitary and ugly place. This is hell on earth I thought.

My new guide, the charming, talkative Indian young woman kept telling me that Sai Baba knows what we think, that he knows our past and future lives, and could perform incredible miracles. He materializes anything with the wave of his hand, a holy ash (*vibhuti*) that heals you physically, emotionally, intellectually and spiritually. I was a hard nut to crack, but I was intrigued and would try to get to the bottom of this phenomenon. Most amazing to me was that they also had a God in the form of an elephant, *Ganesh*. All this was extremely difficult for me to swallow.

I was determined to get to know this character better and get an interview. Why were these bunch of boobs so taken by him? They revered him, they cried just to get a glimpse of him, they rushed to touch his feet. How come I didn't feel anything? My mind kept racing, trying to decipher what Sai Baba is capable of doing. How will I approach him? What's so special about him? The idea that he could tell me the future was most important to me. I was in my 20's and was longing to be able to map out a good life materially, emotionally, intellectually and spiritually. Would he tell me how to achieve this and advise me where to live? How to live? What to do? How to achieve spiritual knowledge? Should I live in the US, France, Honduras, or stay in India forever and dedicate my life to God, becoming a yogi? Would he advise me to study the Vedic scriptures and so forth, so that when I would return to the West I would be someone with knowledge? I could become a spiritual teacher myself.

My goal was to learn more about the mysteries of life. Somehow, I was sure India had answers for me to lead a peaceful life and prepare me for the next life. I had already bought into karma. I found the West chaotic; the war in Vietnam was going on, the Cuban revolution, guerilla warfare in Colombia, the violence of the West, the blacks' struggle for human rights in the US. I disliked the generally aggressive demeanor of Westerners, even the way people walk - Indians stroll gently, Westerners pound the pavement - the huge portions of food that Westerners devoured. I had learned in economics that the surplus of food in the US was thrown into the sea, to stabilize prices - very good for economic theory, but very bad for the starving people in other parts of the world. I thought it was atrocious. I knew that getting more material things did not make me happy. Yes I was a young idealistic Latina wandering to strange lands to find a different path, a different way of life. I was looking for real meaning in the human spirit of this human life.

Here I was in this remote Indian village, in the presence of a spiritual teacher whom I did not understand. I decided that I was going to imitate the yogis who came to the *mandir* and sat in meditation all day long. I got up at 4am, went to the temple and stayed there the whole day. I could not stop my eyes from crying. It is at this time that I realized that I had missed my father all my life. Buckets and buckets of tears ensued. I felt the pain of my existence, the pain of those miserable people outside the gate of the ashram, the pain of so many human beings in the world. I felt so much compassion for humanity. My body was young but everything hurt, my bones, my muscles, my head, my spine, I felt like a 100 years old. Somehow, my silence had allowed me to absorb the heavenly paternal love pervading the *Mandir*.

I felt I finally understood reincarnation and *karma*. I understood that we leave the body and we go into the spirit world where there is lasting peace, but if we still have work to do for our spiritual advancement, we reincarnate and get a new body; we choose our parents, we choose our country, we choose our life on earth. While we're here, we have the opportunity to learn good lessons, and be a good human being, in order to go back to the spirit world and regain that eternal peace. We do bring back knowledge from past lives, and apply it in the earthly plane, perhaps that's why we find that some people are very talented or that some people come for just a little while.

The next day after my catharsis, during morning *darshan*, Baba walks in my direction and materializes *vibhuti* to a lady sitting next to me. Wow! I saw it, but I immediately discarded it as a magic trick. But why didn't he do it for me?

That afternoon *darshan* I concentrated very hard, in my mind's eye telling Baba to please make *vibhuti* for me. He came around, here, there, but he decided to go back to the *mandir*. With my thoughts I was screaming at him: "Didn't I tell you to do it for me?" Amazingly, he read my thought, he turned around and walked directly to me and materialized *vibhuti*. I did not even know what to do with it. Some Indian ladies around me starting taking bits from my hand. Then I got selfish, closed my hand and said: "This is for me, stop taking." I was thrilled. This being could hear my thoughts, even fulfill my desires! I kept writing him letters, pouring out all my emotions, all my convoluted thoughts, all my anger and resentment with the world the way it is.

No One Comes Here Unless I Bring Them

The cultural shock of Puttaparthi was still disturbing me. One morning I spotted an American hippie with long hair, eyeglasses, and the aspect of an intellectual. I went over and asked him: "What are you doing in this miserable place?" I gave him a litany of complaints about the living conditions and my dislike for Puttaparthi.

He looked at me with scorn and said: "Instead of moping and groaning, why don't you read this book?" It was *Man of Miracles* by Howard Murphet. I was more than impressed: I opened the book at random and read: "No one comes to Puttaparthi unless I bring them here." Suddenly it clicked – the car accident, the precipitous trip to India, the coincidences that had brought me here. This generous young American gave me his book. I could not put the book down. All of a sudden, Sai Baba became very important; I had better stop calling him 'this character,' 'this guy.' It dawned on me that he is an enlightened being, that's why people touch his feet.

One evening *darshan*, Baba comes where I am but ignores me completely; as he is leaving I called to him loudly: "Baba, don't you see that I am right here?" He turned towards me and in the sweetest voice he said: 'Be patient, Be patient, Be patient." He gives advice in such a loving way that we melt.

One afternoon Baba comes out of the *Mandir* and calls Mr. Gupta's family to the veranda. Among the children, one was epileptic. Baba waved his hand and materialized a small bottle with a white liquid. At that time I had no idea what *amrith* was. He passed on the bottle to the child's mother and waves his hand again and materializes the instructions and sticks them to the bottle. This was the medication for that child. I open my mouth in disbelief!

Another afternoon, I am sitting in *darshan* and a very elegant lady sat next to me. I recognize that she was French. I asked her: "Vous êtes française, n'est pas?" (You are French, aren't you?) She responded: 'Yes!' "What are you doing in this sort of place?" I asked. She emphatically said: "This is my second trip. This is the most extraordinary place on earth - *Prasanthi Nilayam* (Abode of Peace)." Wow, what a relief! A European's opinion reassured me.

Now, I had to be pro-active and find ways to engage with the Avatar. I had to get an interview no matter how. I realized that Mr. Kasturi was the closest devotee to him. After *darshan* I followed Kasturi to his house. He sat down and started typing so fast with two fingers on a very old typewriter. I approached him very politely. I knew this was a very important person and he could lead me to Baba; I asked him: "Mr. Kasturi, I see you with Baba, you can surely get an interview for me. I come from Honduras, such a remote place, and this is the only opportunity I have. Please tell him to be fair. He calls people who live around here. I have come a long way, this is difficult for me. I am young and would like him to tell me what to do with my life." Kasturi nodded his head and told me that Baba had no intermediaries; he is the only one that calls whoever he wants. No hope with Mr. Kasturi.

That evening *darshan*, Baba approached me and asked my name. I said: "Rosa," he responded: "Do you know what it means?" I said "a rose, like a flower." He said: "No, it means fasting." "Baba. I don't understand." He said it means "fasting of the tongue, fasting of the mind, fasting of the hands, which means, say no evil, think no evil, do no evil." "I like that" I responded. I felt so special. He had talked to me in such a loving way. He penetrated in my heart.

At that time I was taking thyroid pills. The next day as I am to take the pill, I reflected and decided to throw them out and take the *vibhuti* instead. I had to continue engaging with the Avatar. I need that interview, I am impatient. Then I thought: "Baba must eat. Who is the cook?" I asked around and was directed to the back of the *Mandir* where there was a kitchen. A lady came over; I gave her a note for Baba and asked her to place it between the cup and the saucer. I told her it was very important because once he reads that message for sure he will give me the interview. I was obsessed. That is all I could think about.

Somehow, this lady would come to *darshan* to tell me: "Baba says he will see you this afternoon." I was so eager to be called. He would come out and ignore me completely. I was so disappointed. Before leaving I would stop by the kitchen and she would say: "Baba says he will see you tomorrow morning." I could not sleep; I was trying to think of intelligent questions I would pose in the interview, but my mind was blank.

The next day the same performance would be repeated. I was like a yoyo. I had lost all control. I was just observing all the fanatics touch and kiss the wall outside of his room. How come I did not feel anything? All I could do was criticize him, criticize the behavior of these simple-minded people, criticize the living conditions of the place, but I really wanted to feel one fraction of the love some people expressed towards him. My heart was so closed, so hard; I perceived that what really moved me and made me go to a heavenly state were the *bhajans* inside the *mandir*. There was an incredible lady singer, Vijaya, who played the *veena*. When I listened to this music my heart would melt, then I would lie down and let myself go into to a deep, deep relaxation.

Well, I insisted so much on the interview that one evening the lady came looking for me and said: "Baba is going to see you now." She ushered me into a room with one big chair. I thought it was the reception area and sat on the chair. Sitting there, while waiting for Baba, my emotions were turbulent. Now, I was even fearful. "What am I going to ask him?" I had no questions. Finally I relaxed; I was feeling so good that I was not sure why I had insisted so much to have this interview. A long time passed by, maybe an hour. Baba was having dinner upstairs. Then, Mr. Kasturi came down and very lovingly said to me: "Baba says that he is too tired to see you this evening." I felt like a flat tire. I wanted to come back home to familiar territory and have an ice cream cone.

People kept telling me that I could not leave if Baba did not give his permission. "He keeps ignoring me, how am I going to ask for permission?" At that time there was no transportation, but the next day some people arrived in a car. I went over and asked if I could ride back to civilization with them. That night I dreamt that Baba was coming with me in the car and he placed a garland on me. I woke up and interpreted the dream as a sign that I could leave. I had breakfast with Mr. Gupta, told him the dream and he agreed with me. Baba was giving me permission to leave the ashram.

I was alone in that long, long ride back to Madras. I was crying all the way back. I was leaving this incredible, fascinating, loving being for what? I had no emotional or physical endurance. I wanted to see my loved ones, wanted a comfortable life, a shower with warm water, to walk with shoes, eat Western food, and much more.

When I got back to Mrs. Futnani's house, she was eager to hear about my adventure with Baba. She kept telling me: "You are an incredible and daring young woman." I spent one day in Madras with Mrs. Futnani; my only shopping desire was to obtain the most beautiful stainless steel boxes in which to put *vibhuti* and share with family and friends. I still had to go to meet the French mother in Pondicherry. Aurobindo's ashram was clean, well organized, the people very correct, but all I wanted was to go back to Baba. However, I needed to get back to the West.

I was running out of time and decided to go to Delhi to see the Taj Mahal. I was back to being a tourist, facing the shocking overpopulation of India and the contrasts between rich and poor. I decided to go to Agra by train with the vast majority of people and got a third class ticket. I was pushed into the wagon and saw there was no place for me to put my face. Indians have the art of accommodating themselves in a very limited space. I came right out and got into a first class wagon. It is not easy to experience such different worlds. I admired how strong these people are.

My last task was to bring back musical instruments from India – *tamboura*, *tabla*, *sitar*, even a *shruti box*. Indian culture is most accessible to Westerners through its music, which conveys a strong spiritual component. Little did I know that to transport these instruments was going to be more than challenging. At the airport the airline was to charge not only by size but by volume. I needed to clear these instruments with customs. For that I needed to hire a broker. I spent a whole day at the airport in Delhi getting acquainted with the convoluted Indian bureaucracy. Anyhow, I flew with the *tamboura* and the *sitar* (each black box was the size of a coffin), the rest of the luggage came by cargo.

Back to the West

It was very difficult to come back to the West. I felt a knot in my throat, I was leaving this incredible beautiful country with such beautiful people and where I had met this extraordinary being Sathya Sai Baba. My only regret was not to have had the coveted interview. I was nostalgic, I kept remembering every ritual from four o'clock in the morning till evening, and that beautiful ritual he had with Geeta, his elephant. The elephant would put a garland on him, and he would feed and pat it; the elephant was so wonderful, I was feeling tears of joy, and I was so unhappy, he had not patted me at all, I wished he had given me a fraction of attention he does to Geeta.

First miracle at a distance

Upon my return, because there were snowstorms in New York, we were sent to Paris overnight. I was thrilled to get together with friends and specially Chantal's mother. At that time it was difficult for French people to get substantial amounts of money out of France, so Chantal's mother entrusted me with cash for her daughter studying at NYU. I put it in the safest place with my passport and my own money.

Arriving in New York, Maurice meets me at the airport. We take the bus back to Manhattan and I proceed to tell him the story about this incredible being Sai Baba, the *vibhuti* and materializations. He listened and believed every word I said. He had spent a year in India studying classical flute and he knew the mysteries of that land. He observed a real transformation in me, more than even I realized.

When we got home I found that having been so intent on recounting my adventure with the Avatar, I had lost all my documents together with Chantal's money. I simply said: "I don't have to worry about it, Sai Baba will bring it back to me." We went to sleep and sure enough, the next morning I got a call from the bus terminal asking me to come right away and identify myself in order to recover the lost documents. To my surprise, every dollar bill was there!

The first thing I did was set up my *puja* with a picture of Sai Baba when he was very young, with straight hair and a halo, and an expression of pure transparency.

First Sai Satsang in New York

I felt at home in the West enjoying all the material comforts, something that Westerners take for granted. Yet, I was missing this extraordinary being Sathya Sai, and the atmosphere created by the devotees surrounding him. I realized I needed like-minded people. In the ashram I heard there was a lady in New York who in her youth had been a dancer, and had spent nearly 20 years in India; her name was Hilda Charlton. I called her and she was happy to have recent news from India. We spent four hours together. She shared so many stories of so many spiritual teachers she had met in the Himalayas and other holy places; she was a disciple of Swami Nityananda and before coming back to the West she had met Sai Baba. She suggested we get together every Thursday for *bhajans* and meditation.

We were less than half a dozen people. The group got bigger and moved to an apartment on the West side. Again, the group got bigger and migrated to St. Lukes church; a few years later it ended up at St John the Divine, the city's largest cathedral. Hilda included Jesus, Allah, and other spiritual masters in these sessions. She emphasized the importance of positive thinking. She used to say: "Every time a negative thought comes to your mind, you think: cancel, cancel, and cancel." One affirmation that I especially cherish is: "I am God's perfect child, I am happy, I am healthy, I am joy giving" - children love it.

Seek and Ye Shall Find

Since my first trip, *bhajans* were heavenly sounds but foreign and inaccessible; there were no books, and certainly no translations. Early on, we would try to decipher the sounds, syllable by syllable, writing them as we heard them. Our desire to sing *bhajans* was there but at that time it seemed an impossible task for Westerners. Somehow, I heard that there actually existed a long play recording with Baba singing *bhajans*, available in the West. Needless to say we looked for that record in every music store. Nowhere to be found. One day we are strolling in Times Square and we noticed a dingy record shop in the subway entrance of 42nd street and 8th avenue. In all of Manhattan, this was the most unlikely place to find Baba's *bhajans*. We walked in and I moved directly to a pile of records; much to my surprise, behold the wanted record! Swami's *Leelas*. God is everywhere!

New York has its own Guru

In December of 1972 we heard on prime time news: "New York has its own guru." We took the car and went to 86th Street and Central Park West. Sitting on a bench surrounded by a few people was Gil. He was a young ex-marine who had spent some time in India including Puttaparthi. He had the long matted hair of an Indian *sadhu*; he had made a vow of silence, and for several months had installed himself on a public park bench.

A British Shakespearean actor interpreted into words his gestures. Around them there was a constant gathering of spiritual aspirants. As soon as he saw me he gave me a picture of Baba and said "welcome home." I was surprised. Everyone around looked at me and asked me to tell them more about this enigmatic spiritual master, Sai Baba. Every evening we would gather, wrapped in blankets and sleeping bags – after all it was winter. People would bring food, flowers, and books. Gil would never keep anything; he simply gave it away to others. Some wealthy people who admired the group even gave away tickets to go to India. That's how some early Western devotees went to Sai Baba. The gatherings attracted even famous people - Alan Ginsberg, Peter Max were occasional visitors.

Gil's advice to everyone was to "let go." Some understood 'let go' of all possessions; they would announce: "tomorrow we are giving everything away, drop by the apartment and take whatever you want. We are going to India." Gil gave them different names like: 'Now,' 'Rainbow,' 'Sunshine,' 'Precious.' Some of these young people later spent months, even years at Baba's ashram, financed by devotees who worked here and supported them - $100 a month went a long way in Puttaparthi. I remember Helen; she was a school teacher in New York and was continuing studies for her doctorate. Someone gave her my name; she came to visit because she wanted to know more about Sai Baba. Next thing I knew, Helen dropped out and was on her way to India. For years she would come back, be a freelance teacher, save enough money and go back to Puttaparthi for another six months or so.

At some point the group got so large that the New York police very politely but firmly gave a 24 hour notice to disperse. Some members of the group brought a yellow school bus, putting it at Gil's disposal. The next day, 24 hours later, Gil got up, went into a dervish dance, and within half an hour everyone present had to decide whether to get on the bus or not. No one knew where or how far the bus would take them.

Maurice was on the bus, which led to his continuing journey through Mexico, ending up in Colombia with the indigenous people, the Koguis and Aruacos.

Devastating Diagnosis

The summer of 1973 while Maurice was in Colombia, Ofelia, his mother was diagnosed with breast and bone cancer. The doctors told me she had three months to live. I prepared to face the situation by taking seminars with Dr. Elizabeth Kubler-Ross on *Death and Dying*.

That book put her in the limelight as a best-seller author. At that time people used to hide the truth about a terminal illness diagnosis. Dr. Kubler-Ross' argument was that patients know when they are dying, and prefer to know the truth rather than have relatives become actors pretending that everything is fine when it isn't. Patients should be allowed to express their sorrow for leaving loved ones. Also, they need to be able to take care of practical matters before their demise. Dr. Kubler-Ross clearly depicted the five stages that the dying and their families undergo during such trying times. These are: denial, anger, bargaining, depression, and finally resignation to and acceptance of this inevitable situation.

I was working in hospitals and I did service by counseling dying patients about the acceptance of their diagnosis, treatments, and preparation for the final stage. I talked mainly to Spanish and French speaking patients, but doctors would call me to please go and see some English speaking patient as well. I was very moved when I had to help a young patient realize that there was no more hope for living.

In Ofelia's situation, however, my first reaction was that I would go back to the Avatar. My hope was that with the wave of his hand he would materialize a medication, with a second wave the instructions, and I would bring back the miraculous medicine. Had I not seen Baba do something like that for an epileptic boy? Clearly, families go through the stages Dr. Kubler-Ross highlights in her book. At first is denial and we refuse to accept the devastating diagnosis; we think it is a medical mistake. Then, anger takes over. Why in the world is this happening to a dear one? Where is God!

As we realize we have a very sick person in the family, we begin to practice the third stage which is bargaining. If this person can last to a new birthday, till Christmas time, a few more months, and so on. As we begin to get fatigued from facing the situation, at that point, we can most likely become depressed. As caregivers, we have no time for ourselves. No time for entertainment. All you can do is give, give, give. All one can think of is to provide physical comfort, take care of healthy food, administer medications in a timely manner, and lighten up the environment by creating almost a festive ambiance.

Hospital rooms have dull colors, dull paintings. I changed the dull blankets with colorful Bolivian blankets and brought our own paintings. I kept spiritual music playing. Other patients would come by to enjoy the atmosphere created. I wrote to Maurice and miraculously the letter reached him, hand-delivered, high up in the Sierra Nevada de Santa Marta. Maurice returned, and together with our Sai devotees, we did our best to keep a high morale.

At home, our Sai family played music, helped with cooking, read beautiful books. We kept the place immaculate; I made sure we had beautiful flowers. By November I had made up my mind to return to India. To my surprise Ofelia said: "Why don't I go with you?" Mind you, she had never believed any of my stories about Sai Baba; she thought I was a loose cannon, but now she was in a desperate situation and was willing to take a chance. My response was: "Well, if you are going to die anyhow, what difference does it make if it is in New York,

India or Honduras?" I warned her about the lack of comfort in Puttaparthi, but she didn't care. She was intrigued with my loving stories of my wonderful Sai Baba. She had the best medical care New York had to offer, but she was in pain. She was seeking help.

REUNION

Doctor of Doctors

In December of 1973, Maurice, his mother and I embarked to cross the Atlantic. I prayed so hard for Baba not to disappoint us. The interview I had wanted so much was again my priority. How to get it this time? We arrived in Bombay and relaxed at the Taj Mahal Hotel for a few days. Then we flew to Bangalore, and a few days later took the three hour ride to Puttaparthi.

Luckily, the first building for guests had just been completed and we were offered accommodation. The next morning we went to *darshan*. I had a letter telling Sai Baba that I was so happy to be back in *Prasanthi*, that I did not want anything for me. I was only asking him to establish a relationship with the people I had brought to him. Please help and don't let me down. He took my letter and *darshan* was over.

That very afternoon Baba called us for interview and the three of us went into that very special room. My heart was pounding, my legs were shaking. This is it!

Baba is the perfect host. First he addressed Ofelia and he told her in a very loving voice: "Too much pain" … he then materialized *vibhuti*, gave it to her and told her to take a pinch every morning and put it in a glass of water for 15 consecutive days. She should stay in *Prasanthi* for two weeks. "After two weeks, no more pain" he said. He then materialized a locket with his picture on one side and Shirdi Sai Baba on the other side. My God! He did live up to my expectations. He came through in such a beautiful way, I kept telling him with my thoughts how much I love him, how grateful I am. It was a fantasy world. This was indeed "Man of Miracles." How lucky I was to be sitting in front of him.

I was so excited coming out of the interview room that I could even make fun of the locket. I said: "It looks cheap, out of Woolworth. Why doesn't he make something that looks out of Cartier?" Then I felt guilty. What in the world makes me say such a thing? Christmas day Baba called Western women for an interview. Remembering my negative comments about the locket I stayed in the back of the room. As Baba is sitting down, he looked at me and asked: "How did you like the locket?" I said: "Baba, it is beautiful!" He gave me a strong gesture with his arm which I interpreted as saying: "what a hypocrite." Intuitively I raised my arm and something got stuck in the palm of my hand. Everyone in the room sighed. I opened my hand and showed them the locket - identical to the one I had criticized. This locket is still one of my precious possessions. What a Christmas gift! Baba gave me attention!

By 1973, several young adventurous Westerners were staying in *Prasanthi*. Sai Baba had provided them with a shed and gave them a lot of attention. I did not mingle too much because an ashram is a place to go inward, and Ofelia needed my assistance, but I always kept my antennae up to know what is going on in the ashram. I heard Baba was going to go to Rajahmundry for an All India Conference of the Sathya Sai Seva Organization. I was torn between staying with Ofelia and Maurice or following Baba's itinerary. In the last minute I grabbed my few belongings and ran out to get a ride to Rajahmundry - I would meet Ofelia and Maurice in Whitefield upon my return.

I ended up going by train, but on New Year's Eve, trains, buses and taxis went on strike. I was travelling with four American women devotees who in spite of having hepatitis, were eager to attend the conference. We had no choice - back to sleeping on the bare concrete at a train station. Very humble people wanted to share a bit of food. I could not accept because of fear of hepatitis. All night I dreamt that I was in New York having turkey, grapes, cake, and what not. Then my dream moved to Tegucigalpa where they still eat the traditional Mayan nacatamales, cake, apples, grapes - everything so delicious from the West.

The next day we managed to get a taxi and arrived in Rajahmundry. We were given a big room for the five of us. These women who were so sick, they wanted to have the windows closed; they only drank Coca Cola. I tried to open the windows for a bit of fresh air and make tea for them, but they refused.

At the conference we had no credentials to get in. I rushed to the front where Sai Baba and some *pundits* were going to be giving discourses. The *seva dal* tried to hold me back and send me away. I pulled out my locket, showed it to her and said: "This is my pass, Baba gave it to me." She sat me right in front of Baba. He was a great speaker, full of energy with beautiful gestures. The other speakers seemed to be well educated and important people, but I had a hard time understanding their accent. I only wanted to see Baba. I felt he knew I was sitting there admiring him. I had never seen anyone so charismatic.

The trip back from Rajahmundry to Bangalore was difficult; I was trying to take care of the hepatitis ladies, but they would not listen to me.

I feared they could die. Coca Cola was their sole sustenance.

I met Ofelia and Maurice at the hotel. Ofelia was ecstatic because she had no more pain, just as Baba had told her, and we were to see Baba in Whitefield that afternoon.

At that time devotees were so few, barely one line of people; I sat in front so that Baba would see me as soon as he stepped out of his house. Baba called me and the three of us went in. He talked to us for a long time. He was so happy and humorous. He would pat my cheek and repeat: "You are such a good person," "You are such a good person." My self-esteem rose 1000%. I consider myself a good person but to have this acknowledged by the Avatar meant so much for me. I asked him if I could offer the locket to my mother because it was so precious and he said: "yes, yes." He waved his hand and made me a pair of *Shiva lingam* earrings and talked to us about *Shiva*, the deity of cosmic consciousness. I still meditate every day holding these *lingam*s.

I was on Cloud Nine getting out of the interview room. My Rajahmundry travelling companions ran towards me; they were curious about the interview. I shared my joy with them but all I got was: "How can he be so good to you when you were so mean to us." I fired back and said: "Because he knows me, he knows the purity of my heart. All I did was worry about your welfare."

Baba was so gracious to us that he granted six or eight private interviews to the three of us. One day he included Nagamani. This lady was in a wheelchair. She was full of joy whenever she saw Baba. He would always give her a bit of attention in *darshan*. This day, he sits and puts his feet up so that Nagamani could do *padnamaskar*. I asked him discretely if he could make her walk again; he laughed and said: "Nagamani used to play chess with Hitler." We all laughed. I understood that it was her karma to be on a wheelchair.

We became friends with Nagamani. She invited us to her house. Her *puja* room was full of Baba's pictures. She had an arranged marriage when she was an adolescent. A few years later she joined her husband in Germany. He had been ambassador of India to Germany and indeed, she had played chess with Hitler. In spite of her physical condition she was always full of joy.

During interview Baba gives us simple teachings, difficult to forget. He told us: "Be happy, be happy all the time. Live in the present." I thought to myself: "how is that possible?" I usually walk around thinking about the past, and with a big question mark on top of my head about the future. Those simple teachings penetrate our being. The past is gone and the future is uncertain. So, why worry?

Somewhere in another interview he said: "I am your mother. I am your father." I was relieved and reassured - I had a father in Sai. The way he said it got to the depth of my being and tears fell from my eyes. I felt such immense love; I had never experienced Divine Love. It was exquisite.

In one of the interviews Maurice posed so many questions to Baba, about Adam and Eve, Christianity, enlightenment, and so forth. With infinite patience, he would answer the endless questions we had. Maurice had his flute with him, and at one point Baba zeroed in on the flute and said to us: "You see, the body, like a flute, nine holes, a musical instrument offered to God." Baba then started moving his hand and materialized a ring for Maurice; "for *jnana*" he explained. This is a very unusual ring, with a stone of indigo color. He also signed a *Jnana Vahini* book for him and a *Prema Vahini* book for me. Maurice could follow Baba's sense of humor, which often is a play on words. We laughed so much, we were so happy.

Another day in the interview room Baba was so jovial and wonderfully humorous. We all joked around and laughed a lot. Towards the end of this interaction, Baba waves his hand and materializes a calling card for Maurice, with elegant graphic design. He tells him: "Write me, full moon." Since then Maurice dutifully and lovingly writes to Swami every full moon.

A few days later we were called for interview again. Every time, I feel butterflies in my stomach, my heart pumping, my pulse accelerated, and when we finally get into the private quarters of the Avatar, somehow I managed to sit right up front and he gives me the energy to talk to him as I talk to any of my friends. I have seen people who cannot utter a word in his presence.

He asked me: "What do you want?" I said: "Baba, I am in your presence and I feel perfect. I have no desire for anything else." Because Baba is a perfect being, in his presence we feel that we are the most wonderful, loving, compassionate human beings. Yes! We are also perfect. He patted me on the shoulder and said: "Such a good person, such a good person." I was deeply moved by such a flattering comment. Yes! All my life I have struggled to be a good person, to do good things. I wanted my mother and my teachers to be pleased with me. The day before our departure, Sai Baba approached me and asked when we were leaving. I said: "tomorrow Swami." He told us to go into the interview room. I had a big picture of him in my hands and asked him to please sign it. He wrote: "with Love and Blessings, 7/1/74" [i.e. January 7, 1974] and signed it. He was only 48 years old, very dynamic, happy, friendly, and with a tremendous sense of humor.

Back to reality in New York

We had had the most extraordinary trip. Sai Baba was an incredible host; he gave us such good advice and moral support. Ofelia had no more pain, just like Baba had said. She believed she had been healed. Most of all, her trust in Sai Baba opened a new spiritual dimension for her. She was never a religious person. She was a humanitarian, whose entire life was devoted to social welfare and human rights. Religion appeared to her as 'opium for the masses' and an obstacle to social progress. In working with the problem of the millions of displaced persons after World War II, the racial divide in the United States and the living conditions of migrant workers, and family planning programs in Latin America, she often found herself at odds with the conservatism of the Catholic

Church. Her encounter with Sathya Sai allowed her to transcend these political considerations and be fully open to spirituality.

Summer showers in Brindavan 1974

The three of us are now in the Sai fold, but each with our own relationship with the Avatar. By serendipity, the ring that Baba had materialized for Maurice got lost. We looked for it meticulously for a whole month. It seemed the only solution was for him to return to Baba and clarify the meaning of this disappearance. Somehow, we connected with Dr. Sharma who had a travel agency and did some work for the United Nations. He needed help and asked Maurice to help in exchange for a trip to India. We all helped, even stuffing envelopes.

The day of departure, guess what! While packing, Maurice finds the ring in one of his shoes. This was a clear call from Baba, and off he went anyway. He was fortunate enough to be accepted as one of only four Western students to the Summer Showers month-long Course in Indian Spirituality, over which Baba presided over personally. Maurice left as a long-haired hippy, and returned as shaven-head disciple of Sathya Sai. Clearly one of Baba's *leelas*.

Yoga Teachers Training with Indra Devi

By now I was seriously committed to yoga. Indra Devi was my inspiration. She had had an incredible life, from being a Russian princess to a Bollywood film star in India to a famous yoga teacher. She brought yoga to the West. She attracted even Hollywood stars to become yoga practitioners. Most important, she was very devoted to Sai Baba and had access to him. She arranged trips for people who wanted to meet the Avatar.

The summer of 1974 I enrolled at her Sai Yoga Academy in Tecate, Baja California with a group of women who were interested in the yoga teacher's certificate. Part of our yoga course was to have a cleansing diet for two weeks. I volunteered to be the first one. This diet would eliminate all the toxins in the body. It consisted of having eight glasses of water with lemon and chia seeds. I did not want to lose weight and added molasses. I would sit around the dining room, see everyone else eat luscious vegetarian food. I stuck to my pitcher. I had no adverse reaction, just a little fatigue which allowed me to relax, using the hammocks in the beautiful gardens.

As a fellow devotee of Sai Baba, Indra Devi took me under her wing. Along with her adopted Mexican daughter, Rosita, the three of us would go into Indra's meditation room, sing one or two *bhajans*, that's all we knew at that time. At times she would bring me into her bedroom and confide in me the challenges she was facing in maintaining a very expensive yoga academy.

Dr. Knauer, Indra Devi's husband was a theosophist. His lectures were extremely interesting. Just to give you a highlight. One evening he explained to us that as yoga aspirants, through meditation, we were preparing ourselves for telepathic communication with beings from outer space - from the galaxies and the milky way. He was a follower of Rudolph Steiner.

I thought I was to have a lifetime career as a yoga teacher, just like Indra Devi. Some of the classmates opened their own yoga schools. Sharon Sandweiss also took the course and later invited us for dinner to her home in San Diego. As usual, Indra Devi and I would not stop talking about Sai Baba. Sharon's husband, Dr. Sam Samweiss, went on to write *The Holy Man and the Psychiatrist*, perhaps the most instrumental book to introduce Sai Baba to Westerners.

Swami Bua

Back in New York, I learned that there was an Indian *Yogi* living on the West side near Lincoln Center. I immediately went to visit him. I saw his pictures doing the most impressive yoga *asanas* (postures), giving a demonstration to Sai Baba. There he was doing a scorpion pose in front of Sai Baba, who is looking on with an admiring smile, perhaps a teenager at the time. Naturally, I became a regular at Swami Bua's. He actually left me in charge of the yoga school while he went to India on a long sojourn.

I managed very well. Most of my experience was very positive except for one day when a young guy shows up at 10 a.m. and tells me that he is tripping on a hallucinogenic and he felt like jumping from a window. I calmed him down and proceeded to read to him *The Tibetan Book of the Dead*. I was calling on Sai Baba to please give me the wisdom to help this youngster to come back to our real world. After 12 hours we succeeded. He became normal and thanked me.

Death flirting from a corner of the room

Western doctors had given Ofelia a couple of months survival; with Sai's grace this was extended to a couple of years. Nonetheless we had to deal with death flirting from the corner of the room every day. We did this in the most loving and natural way. With the moral support of our fellow Sai devotees we were the best caregivers. Our spirit was up all the time. To keep her entertained Maurice installed a system where she could listen live to all the speakers directly from the General Assembly of the United Nations, this way she was abreast of the socio-political and economic affairs of the world. During this time of remission, she was able to travel to Europe, Africa and Latin America. The crowning event of her career was the first United Nations International Women's Conference, held in Mexico in 1975 which she attended as a delegate representing Honduras.

At some point we had to face the inevitable. In the midst of joking, talking politics, remembering the teachings Baba had showered us with during those incredible interviews, Maurice and I were able to communicate to her that she did not need to keep herself alive because of us, she was free to go whenever she felt ready, and so she did, leaving the body in December of 1975. I kept calling on Baba to give us the strength and help us through this transition. He gave me the courage to sit by her bed, and hold her hand till her last breath. I was alone because Maurice was taking care of practical matters. Her final gaze was staring at a picture of Sai Baba.

Of course I was in shock, but I remembered that in Latin culture, death is not only a tragedy, but a spiritual transition. All Saints Day is festive in Mexico. I had observed a wake and burial with the Mazatec Indians in the mountains of Oaxaca. They sang and played music all along the way to the cemetery, the men in white and the women with their colorful outfits. One must accept and find solace in the fact that our time on earth is a gift and only God knows how and when we will leave the body. We trust our spirit goes to eternal peace, eternal bliss.

The bereavement period, however, is a real struggle. Again, I had to face my feelings about death. Some of my tools were Dr. Kubler-Ross' book *Grief*, and Ruth Montgomery's *The After Life*, as well as the *Tibetan Book of the Dead*. I understood that mourning should not be encouraged, because our detachment is helpful to the spirit of the person during *bardo*, which is a state of suspended reality between death and rebirth.

Seeking Career Change

I had worked in public health for ten years with a modest income. By now I realized that making a living as a yoga teacher was not going to sustain me. I said to myself: "Wake up! You are living in a capitalistic country, learn to make money." I went to the Women's School where they had all kinds of workshops to empower women - personal finance, publishing, advertising, and broadcasting. So, I decided that I should work either on Wall Street or in Broadcasting. In the 70's women were just coming out of their shell. There was one show on television, *Wall Street Week,* where the only presence of a woman was to usher the men into the studio. Very difficult field to penetrate.

So I looked into Broadcasting and realized that a lot of the positions require technical training. I started getting books on this field; *The Cool Fire* was very inspiring. Just at that time we met a French curator of the Metropolitan Museum who along with others was trying to see if Diego Rivera's paintings could be exhibited in New York. Maurice and I got the assignment and off we went to Mexico to meet with the Minister of Culture and the president of the Diego Rivera Museum, Lola Olmedo. We were most impressed by this very strong woman who had been Diego's model since her youth. She

lived outside Mexico City in a huge house.
There were about sixty paintings in her house.
The logistics of the project was complex and
costly. This extravagant project was not realized
till Emilio Azcarraga, president of Televisa and
part-owner of Spanish television in the United
States invested many million dollars to allow
one of the most talented Mexican painters to be
shown at the Metropolitan museum in New
York.

It was natural that we would seek our fellow
bhaktas (devotees) in Mexico City. Dr. Luis
Muñiz and his wife Gail had set up the Sai Baba
Center. They had a bookstore of esoteric books
and a health food restaurant "Yug." We had our
meals there and met very interesting people. It
is in Mexico that I turn on the news and I see a
program *24 Horas* (24 Hours) The anchors were
saluting Spanish speaking viewers in the US. It
was like a light bulb went on. At that moment I
was determined to get a position in Spanish
television in the United States.

I get back to New York, turn to channel 41 and
see a snowy screen, but I am able to have

Mexico in my own living room. How exciting! I was nostalgic; I was missing the sophistication of those people we related to in Mexico. Just by chance, the next day I open the New York Times and see an ad from SIN Spanish International Network. I called the company and requested an appointment with the President. I had learned at the Women's school that one must try to open doors at top levels, because they are the decision-making people within a corporation.

I was given an appointment with the president of Research. He was a real gentleman. After an hour interview he dismissed me telling me that I was very bright but he could not find a position for me at such time. By fluke my resumé ended up at the President's desk, Rene Anselmo, and a couple of days later he had his assistant call me and tell me that he wanted to see me the next day at 10am. I knew this was a Sai leela. I dressed for the part and full of self-confidence went for that type of interview - a job interview, very different from spiritual interviews with the Avatar.

Because my resumé included attendance at a World Conference in Rajahmundry, Rene questioned me about my sojourn in India. He asked me if I knew Gurdjieff. I said I knew of him but not enough. However, I had been in the presence of spiritual masters in India. I told him that I had seen the New York station and it had great potential to educate and inform the Hispanic community, but its programming could improve. I reassured him that I could become an asset to this company.

Then he asked me how much I knew about soccer, about which I knew nothing. This was Friday, he gave me a book about soccer and asked me to come back on Monday and give him a recap of the book. He gave me a tour of the entire office facility and showed me a small round room full of silk cushions. He told me: "This is your meditation room, you can come whenever you feel like it; you can even have a siesta if you feel you need one, because you will be working very hard, you will be working with a World Cup team; you are a good person and I want you to work for this company. So, you start on Monday!"

Waoooooooo.....

I was shaking. How could this man whom I had just met be telling me that I am a good person and offering me a meditation room in a midtown office on 46th Street and Park Avenue in Manhattan? Certainly, a Sai Leela. I was going to give myself a couple of months to look for a job but this was a clear sign from the Avatar. I did not hesitate to accept the offer. I was thrilled to have the soccer legend, Pele, sit next to me and lead me through the first game of World Cup 1978.

I started my new career with a lot of umphhh, with immense enthusiasm and eager to learn more and more about the Broadcasting business. I could never have imagined that within three years I was to become Vice President of Network Sales, and would spend the next 27 years of my life in this fascinating field.

Maurice who had been a French teacher in the best schools in New York was also delving into new technologies. He rented a mainframe computer from IBM. I was in shock when the monster arrived. It was a huge machine that was to take up half our living room. It worked for him but it took away his sleep. He would stay up practically all night fussing with the machine. I did not understand his fascination with computers, they were such dinosaurs. The very same machine today is the ubiquitous small personal laptop.

As I was struggling to be the best salesperson in the company, building my career, I could count my vacation days on one hand; my trips to India were postponed year after year. A tiny picture of Swami on my desk was the extent of my *satsang*.

Swami's Calling Back through the cleaning lady

One day my cleaning lady is on the subway from Queens to Manhattan. She sits next to someone who is reading a book about Sai Baba. She mentions that where she is going to work they have a lot of pictures of this man. She had just met Malini Angunawela who worked at the

United Nations and was president of the Sai Center at the UN.

Malini was very perseverant and started calling us every week to attend the Sai meetings on Friday evenings. Well! People in advertising use those evenings for networking in pubs, bars, restaurants. Friday night is time out!

I kept postponing my attendance to the Sai Center at the UN but every Friday evening I felt unhappy. Deep in my heart I knew I should go to a Sai *satsang*. One day Malini calls and tells me that Dr. Samweiss and Sharon would be at a luncheon and would give a talk about our dear Lord Sai. There was no excuse. I had to attend!

We started attending Sai *Bhajans* on Fridays. Shuba Ramakrishna whose husband was the President of Bank of India lived in the neighborhood. Shuba and her daughter Shanti are the most talented *bhajan* singers. Shuba started teaching us *bhajans*. They became our dear friends.

A Yogi at our doorstep

Another strong sign, which I interpreted as Sai calling us, was an uninvited guest. One morning at 7:30 a.m. our doorbell rings. Lo and behold! An Indian *sadhu* in an orange *dhoti* is on our doorstep. I had met Yogi Shanti eleven years ago when I was teaching yoga at Swami Bua's school.

By coincidence, we had another guest, Laurent, Maurice's 8 year old nephew from Paris. There we were with the most incongruent pair of guests. Yogi Shanti had recently come out of a 40 day fast. He had come to the West to demonstrate to scientists yogic powers, such as transforming the body into pure light.

Laurent only spoke French but he captured everything the Yogi would communicate. The Yogi would tell stories to the child, telling him that after his body was transformed into light, he would come back and take him to visit other planets. When Laurent got back to Paris, Maurice's sister Nicole called us. She was frantic. How in the world did we allow this Yogi to put these things in Laurent's head?

Now he says he is going to go to other planets. We laughed, but reassured her that her child had been well taken care of, not to worry.

Yogi Shanti would wake me up at 4 a.m. to meditate. Imagine! I had to work! To me it was Sai Baba calling us, and we began making plans for a trip at Christmas.

Since my discovering Sai, my mother, a Catholic turned Evangelist, had listened to my adventure with the Avatar but would warn me: "Beware! There are false prophets." I explained to her, over and over, that people of all religions follow Sai Baba's teachings. I wanted her to be blessed by the Avatar. I invited her to join us, but she was undecided. By November of 1989 I had to pay for the airline tickets; I called her with an ultimatum but she answered: "Thanks but no thanks!"

I was disillusioned and asked Sai for a sign. It occurred to me that she should send someone to represent her. This way she would hear not only my story but someone else's as well. I thought one of my brothers could take her place. My eldest brothers were already married. The youngest one, Jorge, was just finishing university. I called my mother to tell her about my new idea. That very morning, Jorge had told her how foolish she was to reject a trip to India. If he had an offer like that, he would instantly accept, and so it was that Jorge had the opportunity to meet Sai Baba.

Trip with the UN Group

At first, Maurice and I announced to the UN group we were going for Christmas to have Sai *darshan*. Malini said: "I'll join you," and so more people were added and we ended up being a group of ten.

On our way to Bombay, we arrived in Paris at breakfast time, had all day in Paris, so we went to meet Nicole and Laurent for lunch. At the end of the day we kissed goodbye to our French relatives and were on our way to meet our Beloved Sai. How exciting!

Upon our early morning arrival in Bombay, we went to a hotel near the airport so we could relax before taking off for Bangalore at the end of the day. We negotiated the use of rooms during the day. We were all jet-lagged, but I wanted to go out to lunch to the Taj Majal hotel. I recruited Maurice, Jorge, and Terry McLuhan, daughter of Marshall McLuhan, the well known media genius who wrote *The Medium is the Message*.

We enjoyed our outing and got back to the hotel just to learn that the hotel manager was reneging on the rates he had given us earlier. I was appalled and out of nowhere said: "Don't do that to us, I am *Durga*!" Well! It did have a lot of impact on this man; he went flat on the floor in *padnamaskar*. He humbly said he was honoring the rates provided to us in the morning. On the way to the airport we were laughing. For someone from Honduras I certainly knew how to deal with people in India.

Christmas was around the corner and the ashram was getting crowded. We were given a room for five women for a couple of days, but then we were given better accommodations. Maurice and I had a room. Jorge, my brother chose to stay in a big Western shed. He had never shared sleeping room with anyone, so this was an experience to be among lots of people.

We enjoyed Christmas. By New Years some in the group had stomach problems. I went to the town, bought a lot of potatoes, salt and butter, went to Monica Muñiz, who had a room with a kitchen, and boiled the potatoes; my travel companions thought it was the most sumptuous dinner.

Darshan after *darshan* and Baba would not call any of us for interview. Only Maurice and I and Malini had had interviews with Baba in the past. I kept telling them to be proactive, think of ways to approach Baba. They would tell me: "Rosa, don't you get it! It is inner-view not interview that matters," even though they had never had the experience. The days went by and we had two days left; I send a telegram to Baba from the town, telling him that I had invited my brother and that an interview with him would be an unforgettable experience for a young man from Honduras.

That night I had a dream with Baba giving orange *saris* to the women and *dhotis* to the men. That morning I got up at 3 a.m. and went to meditate outside Baba's room. I was praying for him to talk to us, give us some guidance. I told our group about my dream. The time comes to go and wait for *darshan*. Somehow I ended up sitting by myself. I had ended up positioned in third row. I could see our group on the opposite side. The person in second row moved up, I took second row, and then the person in front got up and left.

All of a sudden I have front seating. Baba comes out with his majestic walk, comes towards where I am. A group of Argentineans were nearby and they asked aloud: "Swami, Swami, interview please?" Baba asks them "How many?" I believe they said twenty. Baba answered: "Too many." I seized the opportunity and said to him: "Baba, we are only ten from the United Nations group, take us!" He lovingly said: "Go!" I moved fast and my friends followed me. Maurice and Jorge woke up and went up to the veranda. My heart was coming out of my chest, poom, poom, poom!

I saw the men of our group on the veranda. Baba gave a hug to Maurice but sends him back. I felt terrible that Maurice would not be included in the interview, but Baba dismissed him in a loving way. Jorge my brother got in.

Swami's sweetness and immense love makes us melt in his presence. We all sat on the floor. I was near him, Malini beside me. She starting rubbing Swami's feet and he said: "no shoe shine" and we all laughed. Malini had confided in us her wish to have a pair of pearl earrings. At some point during the interview Baba starts waving his hand and materializes a pair of pearl earrings right in front of her, but he proceeds to offer them to a lady sitting next to Malini. Swami's test is palpable. He scolded a young couple; he told them to stop fighting and proceeded to make a small *Shiva Lingam* for them. They were from Venezuela. There was an elderly Indian couple and he materialized a watch for the gentleman. There were three Hindu *sadhus*; Baba went into the inner room and brought them orange *dhotis*. I could not believe that what was happening that morning was a replica of my dream. Swami's *Leelas*!

He called into the inner room the Indian couple, the *sadhus*, and then he called the rest of us. He asked Jorge, my brother to sit in front of him, and proceeded to put his feet on top of Jorge's knees, where he kept them throughout the whole interview. Every so often he would touch Jorge's cheek and talk to him. Violet from our group had lost her husband not long ago. She asked Baba: Where is my husband? He said: "He is with me."

The Spanish group was rehearsing Spanish *bhajans* with the hope of singing in the *Mandir*. The Venezuelan asked Baba if he would allow us to sing the next day. Baba said: "Yes! Yes!"

Interview is over; I let everyone get out of the room. I was the last one, Baba is ushering us out. Then, I asked: "Baba, will you give interview to the men that you sent back this morning?" He said "yes!" Then, I begged, "this afternoon, Baba?" He responded: "Yes!"

I ran out and told Maurice that Baba was to call him in the afternoon, to make sure he would be impeccably dressed.

That was one of the most exciting days for me in *Prasanti*. Sure enough, that afternoon, Baba calls Maurice. I see him get up, and then I ran towards the *Mandir*. To my surprise no one else in the group got up, not even Jorge, my brother.

We went in with a young Indian couple and a few others. In one day I saw so many materializations! He was so generous! I was so happy that Maurice had a chance to interact once again with Baba. Towards the end, referring to Jorge, my brother, he says to Maurice: "Bring him to me, tomorrow."

As we are coming out of the interview room Baba asked me: "You are singing Spanish *bhajans* this afternoon?" I panicked: How in the world was I going to look for the scattered Spanish singers, get into our white *saris*, get our act together within one hour? I said: "Baba, that's not what you said this morning, you said tomorrow afternoon." I was relieved when he answered: "*Acha*! Tomorrow afternoon."

The next day was our last day in *Prasanthi*. Maurice got a chit from the office to be in front row with Jorge and comply with Swami's request. However, the *Seva Dal* would not allow the two of them to pass, the chit was for one person. Maurice hesitatingly offered it to Jorge and he sat in the back. Well, Baba passed by and did not call Jorge.

I had told everybody to get ready to sing in the *Mandir* that afternoon. We looked like angels, dressed in white. We were waiting outside as a group. All of a sudden I hear people whispering that the Spanish group is not to sing. Instead, the German group has been scheduled. Everyone started doubting, but I was firm and said: "Baba told me we would sing this afternoon. Don't give up!" It was a very hot afternoon, sitting in the sand waiting for *darshan*. Without dismissing us, Baba, in his car, leaves the ashram. Some devotees gave up, needed to drink water, rest in the shade, what not. Was *darshan* over? Unexpectedly, Baba returns, and signals for both the Spanish and German group to enter the *mandir*. Finally, both groups were to sing to Baba, alternating, one German song, one Spanish song.

This was our lesson in perseverance. In fact, a Guatemalan young man who had already spent six months in the ashram trying to get over the loss of his father and had been assiduously rehearsing with us was among those that gave up. When he was back in his room he heard our singing through the loudspeakers, but he could not even get out of his building, the door was locked.

Maurice was sitting with the lead singers at the foot of Swami's chair. As Baba walks in, he scolds him, saying: "Rowdy, didn't I tell you to bring him to me?" Clearly, we should follow his instructions no matter what the obstacles.

Baba enjoyed our performance. Jack Lenchner had wanted to video the event but was not allowed to bring his camera. Once we are inside the *mandir*, Baba walks down the aisle and asks Jack: "Where is your camera?" "Outside, Baba." "Go, bring it!" Jack ran out, brought the camera and proceeded to record the event holding the camera aloft. We would even have a souvenir of the event. It was our last evening; the taxi was waiting outside for us to go to Bangalore. Swami's *Leelas* – every trip is special.

LEELAS

Leelas at Simi's

In the summer of 1983, we were visiting Maurice's sister and nephew in France. Laurent by now was a teenager, and Maurice decided to take him sailing to instill discipline. In the meantime I had to come back to work and I found myself on August 30th, my birthday, utterly frustrated in New York. All my friends were away, and I was by myself. I was lucky to get a phone call from Yogi Shanti, who asked me: "what are you doing tonight?" I said "nothing special, I'm so frustrated and on top of it all it's my birthday" and he said "well, why don't you come to dinner with me? There's an apartment on East 72nd Street where all of Baba's pictures are full of *vibhuthi*." I was so excited; I had seen materializations in India, but never in New York. So we went at six o'clock. A few people were singing *bhajans*, and all the pictures had *vibhuthi*. I was stunned. Amazingly, written on the window sill, in *vibhuthi*, it said: "Sing Bhajans, Sai." Needless to say, henceforth *bhajans* became an integral part of our lives.

When Maurice came back, I was very happy to take him to experience these 'visiting cards' right here in Manhattan. How extraordinary, we were like children. We did not want to impose on this family, but we asked: "do you mind if we come every Sunday at 5 p.m. to sing and to meditate for a little while?" "You are welcome" said Simi, the lady of the house, "but I will be at work." So for the next few months, every Sunday, Reetu, their five year old daughter, would open the door and the three of us held *satsang*. That was the beginning of what would become a stream of Swami's *leelas* over the next twenty years, and a deep friendship with Simi.

Soon after, Simi looked for a house in Larchmont, and the family moved there. From the apartment in New York, she didn't know how to transport the main picture that was full of *vibhuthi* and *amrith*. Incredibly, as mysterious as the manifestation of *vibhuthi*, the picture got transported, and showed up in a particular room of the new house.

One day we decided to have a *puja* on a Sunday morning. The priest called from New Jersey to let us know that there was a problem with his car and he could not make it. We had prepared everything for the *abhishekam* and I said to Simi "well, why don't you and I just simulate that we are doing the *puja*; we have the flowers, incense, yogurt, honey; we can repeat the *gayatri mantra*," and so we did. There were a few other people in the room, mainly from Scarsdale and Larchmont. We finished our ritual and had *prasad*. After that we went back into the room and I saw that in the jar of *vibhuthi*, something was sparkling in it. I realized that something had materialized, pearls! I started spooning them out, little ones, larger ones, oh my God! We were all very excited and amazed. Imagine! Having actual pearls materialize in our presence. We all kept a few, but most of them were given to the mother of a young girl who had autistic problems. Simi decided that a little necklace should be made for this child.

Satsang gatherings at Simi's were very special; some people would take pictures which would get covered with *vibhuti*, *kumkum* or *amrith*. I would bring one of my pictures and I would say to Baba "if I am doing things right, will you make *vibhuthi* in my picture?" As we were singing *bhajans*, I started seeing which pictures would get *vibhuthi*, something cloudy would appear in the background; when that happened, I was certain that picture would get *vibhuthi*. Swami's *Leelas*. Exciting times.

One day we decided to have *akhanda bhajans* at Simi's house, but we were only about six people. I thought 'how are we going to sing for 24 hours, just six of us?' so I invited this friend from Venezuela who was a classical guitarist. I thought: at least that can give us a break, at six in the morning we would finish the first part of twelve hours, he would give us a one hour classic guitar concert, and then we would go on. As a back-up, in case we got exhausted, we had a set of cassettes. By two o'clock in the morning our energy level was dwindling, when all of a sudden the door opened and two wide-awake devotees walked in. One of them began singing a *Shiva bhajan* with so much gusto, it energized us all. Early morning a few Indian families dropped by, and I noticed a shadow in Baba's picture; a few hours later, as we concluded the *akhanda bhajan*, sure enough, to everybody's astonishment, that picture was full of *vibhuti*. Swami's *Leelas*.

One afternoon, while singing *bhajans*, a ring materialized on a picture underneath the glass.

We were so excited, but we finished the *bhajans*. When the *bhajans* were over, we took the picture to the kitchen and opened it; it was a man's ring. All the men that were present tried it on, sure enough, only the owner of the house, Simi's husband, had a perfect fit. Obviously it was for him. Swami's *Leelas*. Exciting visiting card!

At a *puja* for Father's Day, a coconut was opened, inside there was a small deity. In Simi's *puja* room there was a small *lingam*, smaller than my hand; over a period of ten days, it grew, and grew, and grew, to a much bigger size, perhaps tenfold. The picture, the original one from the New York apartment, continued to get *vibhuthi*, *amrith* and *kumkum*. People would come with a lot of reverence to this house.

One time when we went to visit Simi, she was all excited - on a statue of Lord Shiva in the *puja* room, Baba had appeared in miniature, standing on Shiva's head. She asked Baba if she could take a picture, and she actually took a Polaroid picture that she was able to show us. It was right there, unbelievable, Baba standing on Shiva's head. Swami's *Leelas*. How thrilling to see such things.

There was a devotee who needed a kidney transplant. She was looking for a donor. Her parents didn't qualify; her only brother became the donor. In the meantime we decided to do an all night *bhajan* for her. That night, by 11 o'clock, for sure, *kumkum* and *vibhuthi* started appearing on Baba's picture and the *lingam*, which was in a silver tray, started pouring *amrith*, which was offered in spoonfuls to her. What a gift.

The next morning, driving back, she and another devotee are in the back of the car, and we hear them talking as if they had doubts about what had happened. My God, how could they doubt what they had just experienced? I just turned around and said "I can't believe you guys are doubting what you've seen with your own eyes." Two days later I get a call from her, and she tells me that her mother has informed her that in their apartment in Chicago, *vibhuthi* is materializing in Baba's pictures. Swami's *Leelas*.

Simi had moved from Manhattan, to Larchmont, to Scarsdale. Manifestations followed in all three places. She loved having *bhajans*, and *pujas* on special occasions, gathering friends and neighbors. Among these were some of the members of the UN Sai center. Somehow, it got to the hierarchy of the organization that something unusual and perhaps inappropriate was going on at Simi's house, so they sent a letter that they were coming to supervise. There had been complaints, alleging that Simi claimed her house was a 'healing center,' and had been charging money. Outrageous, of course.

The day of the visit happened to be Earth Day, and at UN headquarters there were thousands of flowers which were going to be thrown out at the end of the day. So we took all those beautiful flowers in a van; every room at Simi's house was full of flowers. When the people from the organization arrived, they were amazed. Then they sat down and we discussed the situation. Maurice was the most vocal defendant of Simi. I simply said she is nothing but gracious, she has never charged any money. On the contrary, she has always been very generous to everyone that comes to her house, offering *satsang* followed by *prasad*.

Simi was a very special person. As a nurse she chose to work night shifts so that she could help the dying patients, and the emergency room where the most drastic cases are rushed in. As a householder she was a dutiful and loving mother, but most of all, she was an ardent Sai devotee. I am so happy we were able to be faithful to our dear friend.

Classical concerts on Baba's Birthday.

Maurice's love and fascination with Indian classical music led him to organize concerts at the United Nations to dedicate to Swami on his birthday. Maurice had originally gone to India in 1967 in pursuit of its music. In his last year at Columbia University he took a course in Oriental Humanities. One day Surya Kumari, a well-known classical dancer and singer from Madras gave a workshop, which inspired Maurice to go to the country where that mystical music comes from. A year later he was on a boat from Brooklyn to Bombay.

So now, in 1992, Maurice was trying hard to find the very best Indian classical singer to perform at the Dag Hammarskjold auditorium at the United Nations. This seemed to be an expensive proposition, and as we know, whenever there are Swami's events there is no money involved. The circumstances surrounding this effort show how Swami operates. We think we offer something to him; instead he offers to us a hundred-fold.

For the past year I was looking for a bigger apartment to buy. Prices had skyrocketed and it seemed like mission impossible to stay in the neighborhood we love, Tudor City, right across from the UN.

Many years prior, Maurice had mentioned to the upstairs neighbor that should he ever intend to leave that apartment to let us know. Ten years had gone by and Françoise, a French neighbor knocked on the door and told Maurice that Jacques, our upstairs neighbor had mentioned to her about our interest during a dinner conversation. She came to let us know that Jacques who had retired in France had passed away; his 92 year old mother wanted to settle his estate and was eager to sell the apartment.

We looked into the logistics of it, called the French lady, gave her an offer and she immediately accepted. For me, whose work was to negotiate with clients, this was the easiest negotiation ever. The next day she calls to let us know that the she is being offered twice the amount, and in cash. My answer to her was: "I thought French people were honorable, we had an agreement. We will come up with the cash but stick to the negotiated price." She was so sweet and said to us: "You are very nice people, you knew my son, and I want you to keep the apartment." To make the story short, lawyers decided to do the closing on November 19th. A few days later, they called and said the closing was to take place on November 23, at 4pm. On Swami's birthday! What a coincidence. We attended the closing and rushed to the UN where the Dag Hammarshold auditorium was full to capacity. Swami's *Leelas*.

While we were making a real estate move, Maurice was frantically trying to get a performer for the concert. Someone suggested Lakshmi Shankar, a top classical Indian singer – her voice is featured in the film *Gandhi* – and a Sai devotee. By telephone she told us she was going to Calcutta to an international festival; she would call the airline to see if it was possible to come from Los Angeles to New York and go on to India. The next day she called; the airline had changed her travel plans, allowing her to perform on Baba's birthday. Swami's *Leelas*.

We were so honored to have Lakshmi Shankar as our guest on this and other occasions. She became a dear friend. I have a tremendous admiration for the discipline of accomplished artists like Lakshmi. In India musical training is akin to spiritual *sadhana*. Lakshmi trained her voice seven hours a day, seven days a week, for many years. In one of her trips to New York she was performing at Lincoln Center. She stayed with us and for me to hear her voice doing warm-up exercises was heavenly.

The upstairs apartment became Swami's meditation room. Whenever I went to *bhajans* that took place in people's basements I thought to myself. "Why do they choose the basement to give to Swami?" I visualized a meditation room with only one picture, life size, and of course, we offered the best room to Swami, with a view to the park and incredibly quiet, an oasis in mid-town Manhattan.

Another concert was at the Lighthouse. Maurice managed to get Ravi Coltrane, son of the famous jazz musician John Coltrane, who in his career had sought to integrate jazz and Indian classical music. It occurred to me that in the auditorium behind the performers a large screen could display the film *Pure Love*, a slow-motion depiction of Swami walking among devotees and giving *padnamaskar*; the combination was magical. Alice Coltrane, Ravi's mother was a fervent Sai Baba devotee, a gifted musician, and a spiritual guide, with an ashram in California.

Yogi Shanti's visits...... a reminder of satwic living

Yogi Shanti became one of our dearest friends. He traveled all over the world but managed to come and stay a few days with us a few times a year.

I always enjoyed his eccentricities. Yogi's cooking was *satwic*. He loved the telephone and camera. People would call him and he would call people from all over the world at any time, day or night.

Shukanadi readings

In one of his trips to the U.S. Yogi Shanti decided to bring a renowned *vedic* astrologer. He called us from Haridwar and asked if they could stay with us. I was not very enthusiastic; he insisted and I told him that the two of them could stay for a weekend. Well! That weekend was prolonged to a month. I felt so embarrassed to have been reluctant at complying with Yogi's request. The astrologer, Ramakrishna was a 38 year old man, extremely gentle and well educated. He was also a Sanskrit scholar. His father had done an extensive reading for Sai Baba, featured in the book *Living Divinity*. I survived only because there was never a dull moment. These two characters provided non-stop *satsang* and unique entertainment for us.

Yogi Shanti set up appointments with diplomats and presidents of corporations. I could not believe how interested people were in this type of reading. They set up shop in our living room.

At the end of the first day, I walked into our apartment and I did not know where to put my face. It was packed! The astrologer and the yogi had moved into the bedroom. I conceded only if they allowed me to observe and listen to the readings. Also, I set up standards; there were no money transactions to take place in our residence. If people were generous they could leave a contribution. I was stunned. Ramakrishna was even doing readings over the phone for people from Switzerland, France, Italy, England, Los Angeles, San Francisco and many other places. Yogi Shanti and Ramakrishna were invited to different places throughout the United States, Canada and Europe.

Yogi Shanti was a natural for networking and public relations. He knew so many spiritual leaders. When Amachi would come to New York, he would invite me and I was so busy at work I often declined, but he would insist. "If you come I will get you to hug Amachi in five or ten minutes" Sure enough, there he was with the Indian Consul or ambassador and we would be ushered in. Yogi Shanti would be invited to

Deepak Chopra's seminar and he would bring us along. We met many interesting people through him.

Going to Kodaikanal we end up in Peru

I had always wanted to go to Kodaikanal, a retreat in the mountains where Sai Baba goes usually in April. Because April and May are the busiest time of the year in broadcast business - this is the time when billions of dollars are negotiated in the advertising world - I could not take time off, but I managed in 1996 to plan a trip to Kodai. That particular year the rumor was that Swami would not be going. I pushed forward because I thought it would be wonderful to be with Swami in a resort setting, staying at the comfortable Carlton Hotel.

We had reservations and were ready to go, but at the end the signals for not going that year were too strong. I was disappointed, exhausted from work and needed a break. I thought: If we could not make it to Kodaikanal, at least we should go to get energy from a mountain. Should we go to the Rocky Mountains? Suddenly, I realized we had never been to

111

Machu Pichu, an Inca archeological site in the Andean mountains.

Very quickly we made arrangements to go to Peru; it was just at the time of political turmoil - the Japanese embassy had been taken over by insurgents - but we thought "We are guided by Baba" and off we went. We stayed in Lima, the capital, just long enough to visit museums. I was impressed by the earthy, elegant colors at the textile museum. Peru had a president of Japanese origin, Fujimori. The airport was inundated with Japanese businessmen and tourists in the low lands but they did not go to the mountains.

Sacred Valley of the Incas

We flew to Cuzco, stayed at a monastery converted into a hotel. The first thing one notices in Cuzco is the impressive construction of the Incas using huge rocks. The colonial Spanish construction was right on top of the Inca. We went to a different town every day, becoming familiar with the "Sacred Valley of the Incas."

The altitude of 8,000 feet gave me "soroche" - a slight headache, ringing in the ears, and fatigue. Most tourists are affected by this condition. In the hotel lobby there are baskets full of coca leaves and hot water. One should drink coca tea upon arrival, for our lungs to adjust to that altitude.

Cuzco is one of the most interesting places on earth. The locals cultivate potatoes, quinoa and other types of food. The people up in the mountains look like Tibetans, the children with their rosy cheeks, flowers in their heads, and colorful woolen embroidered outfits.

Our goal was to explore Machu Picchu, the most important Inca archeological site. From Cuzco one takes a train that zigzags down the mountain. Most tourists just go for a quick tour and lunch, but we wanted to experience these stunning mountains, Huayna Picchu and Machu Picchu. We stayed three nights and four days.

Maurice had gone into a bookstore in Cuzco and he met someone with a doctorate in anthropology who had a picture of Sai Baba in his office and who strongly recommended that in addition to taking the historical tour of Machu Picchu, we should take the spiritual tour. For that we needed to locate an Indian (i.e. indigenous American) called ChuChu.

The first day we explored the ruins with a guide who had a PhD in history. We asked for ChuChu but no one knew him. The second day we were ready to climb the mountain on our own. We started early morning and climbed part of the mountain. At some point we realized that for such adventure one needs a guide from the area. As we come back to the hotel, we see an Indian with his woolen hat and outfit and a mochila full of coca leaves. We asked him if he knew ChuChu. To our amazement he answered: "I am ChuChu." We introduced ourselves and told him he had been highly recommended to us by the professor in Cuzco. We asked him to please guide us to the mountain top.

Crawling like a worm to reach the mountain top

That morning we got up at sunrise and luckily we were allowed to enter the ruins. I meditated in the Temple of the Sun. I asked Baba to give us a proof of his presence in that place. Why not make a rainbow for us? I had read that he had done it for an early devotee from California.

Now, we had a knowledgeable native guide whom we trusted. I tried to sell the tour to other tourists but they declined. Even strong men were intimidated to undertake such a climb. I wanted ChuChu to earn a bit more money. In the end one lady from Lima, Maurice and I joined ChuChu to reach the mountaintop. It is a unique experience. There was enough room for one person at a time. The vegetation was so thick one could not see how far we had to go. Every so often ChuChu would offer coca leaves to give us energy. At some point there was the biggest rock I have ever seen. Below the rock there was a crevice. ChuChu told us we had to crawl beneath the rock to come out to the other side. I always call on Sai Baba and remember

115

what he tells us; "Do not fear that I am here." I was bargaining with him. In my mind I was remembering that our original intention was to be with him in Kodaikanal. Instead, look where we were, crawling like a worm or a snake in order to reach the mountain top. Well! We did it! We continued a bit further and came up to the most glorious view of these two mountains. We were high up above the clouds.

Swami materializes two rainbows in Machu Picchu

Overwhelmed by this beauty, this high altitude, we remain quiet. ChuChu tells us that in 15 years he had not seen these mountains in such a clear view. We are sitting on a huge rock, I take a few pictures, and all of a sudden a vertical rainbow forms in the sky. "Look! Baba just materialized a rainbow for me," I cried aloud. Suddenly another rainbow identical to the first one is formed. Again, I cried aloud. "Look! Mo, he just did one for you too." Two rainbows side by side was most unusual.

We were in a heavenly neighborhood, and Baba's presence was strongly felt. What a gift. I am convinced the Avatar is omnipotent and omnipresent.

The next day, I put together a group of ten people, mainly from Argentina, Uruguay, and Brazil to take the spiritual tour of Machu Pichu. ChuChu took us to different sites in the ruins. For the ritual he had incense, candle, camphor, wooden sticks, coca leaves and grains. He started praying in Quechua (the language of the Incas). He explained to us that in each site it was de rigueur to pray to the Gods and ask permission to the Pancha Mama (mother Earth) to proceed with the ritual, similar to a *puja*. Pointing to crevices in the rocks, he revealed that some of those huge stones actually open up to allow spiritual energies to enter the earth below. There was no doubt that we were at a holy site, worthy of our pilgrimage.

Visiting Cards at Shyla's

In the summer of 1998 we were hosting the UN center in our place due to restrictions at the UN for security reasons after the first terrorist attempt at the World Trade Center. Every Friday we would meet at 6pm for *bhajans* and study circle. The study circle discussions, with the participation of an ex-IBM executive, a PhD candidate and the like, would sometimes extend well into the night. Shyla, a devotee from Nyack, NY, attended one of these sessions. When she learned that we were looking for a place to rent while doing substantial construction work to incorporate the upstairs apartment as a duplex, she offered that we stay in her house while she was going to visit Sai Baba. The house is in a beautiful setting by the Hudson River, and the daily commute to Manhattan during Autumn offered a splendid display of colors.

When Shyla got back from India, we set up an altar in the living room, where every day we would sing *bhajans*. Maurice would play the flute, creating a meditative ambience. I had brought one of my favorite Baba pictures, already covered with *vibhuti*. Shyla decided we should have a big *bhajan* and I should help her invite Sai devotees. She started cooking Thursday evening for a Saturday *bhajan* that would be from 6am to 6pm. The home made *prasad* (food) was exquisite. When people left we noticed *vibhuti* had materialized in Baba's chair.

That winter Maurice and I went to visit family in Honduras for Christmas. I left my dear, dear Sai picture with Shyla; she had grown fond of that image of a young Baba. We returned to New York on January 6th. The next day there were six inches of snow on the ground. That late afternoon Shyla calls to let us know that vibhuti and kumkum had materialized on the deities in her puja room. Even with a snow storm we drove up to rejoice in this phenomena. The energy in the room was phenomenal. I was stupefied. Baba's presence was palpable.

Most unusual visiting card

Shyla decides to have another *bhajan*. We had as a guest of honor, Swami Bua, who was over a hundred years old, to play the conch. The *bhajan* started on a Saturday evening. I believe it was *Dasara*. The place got packed. Simi and I were tending the incense, candles, and flowers. We noticed that the main picture in the altar was getting cloudy. Maurice and Swami Bua drove back to Manhattan, but Simi and I asked Shyla if we could sleep on the floor next to the altar, expecting *vibhuthi* to materialize.

That night I could not sleep; every so often I would open my eyes to see if it had happened. Nothing happened all night. The next morning we put the house in order. Simi had to go back to work. Shyla had a luncheon in the city. I was coming back to the city with Shyla at about noon. As I am getting into her car, I decided to go and say goodbye to Baba in the altar. Bending over, I lift my head, and *vibhuti* materializes. I rushed to tell Simi and Shyla; they came into the room, and paid obeisance, but they had commitments and had to leave. I, on the other hand, was exhausted and just felt that I needed to stay and meditate in front of that altar. I called Maurice who was in the city to tell him what had happened and to come and fetch me later that afternoon.

Vibhuti materializes on the pillows

I meditated for a long time. It is an experience that no words can explain. I started getting very sleepy. I go upstairs; see the guest room, then Shyla's bedroom. This room was very inviting; it was plush with white duvet and white pillows. I decided I would lie down on her bed. I picked up two books, one was *Baba and I* by Hislop. The other one was a very small book, with quotes from Baba. As I am reading the sentence "It is not enough that you love me, but you must see that I love you," I felt a strange presence, looked over to the right and beheld *vibhuti* materializing on the white pillows. I could not move. I was stupefied. I did not dare to continue reading; alone in that huge house, I cannot explain how I felt.

A couple of hours later, the phone rings, a close friend devotee called, I told her what happened and she drove up from Manhattan to witness another Baba *leela*. Maurice also arrived from the city, but stayed downstairs, thinking I was asleep. Shyla calls from the road, and asks me: "What are you doing?" I said:" I am in your bedroom, and you won't believe what has happened." When she got home she joined Maurice to contemplate the altar, then both went upstairs and I signaled to the pillows covered with vibhuti. Their faces were of complete total astonishment. Coming back to the city I was in Cloud Nine but had to come down real fast for a Monday 8 a.m. sales meeting.

Gallery with Baba's footsteps in vibhuti and kumkum

Sometime later, Shyla calls and tells us to drive up - Baba's footprints, in *vibhuti* and *kumkum*, have appeared on the wall and floor of the meditation room, extending to the foyer and stairway! We arrived to contemplate this new *leela*. How to preserve this visiting card? Well, each footprint was protected with an acrylic frame. It looked like an art gallery. People would visit as in a museum. Simply awesome!

Another bhajan, another visiting card

Shyla was gracious and invited many devotees to another *bhajan*. Somehow, as soon as the singing was over, a devotee asked me to take her to the upstairs meditation room. We sat there for hours talking to each other about our Beloved Sai. I enjoyed her sincerity and devotion. She told me her entire story with the Avatar. Here was someone with all the Western comforts yet she was always eager to go visit Swami.

By the end of the evening when most people had left, just before coming back to the city I said: "Let me go and say goodnight to Baba." I walked up to the meditation room, bowed down in reverence, but as soon as I finished, I sensed something. I look up to a picture on the left side of the wall, and *kumkum* (auspicious powder) appears. I go downstairs all excited to announce another visiting card.

Saraswati amrith

I wanted to have a *puja* in our own meditation room. A Hindu priest was called. I placed a small statue of *Saraswati* (Goddess of Wisdom) on a large stainless steel tray. Simi brought her friend Chandra, whose husband was hanging between life and death for the past five months. When we finished the *puja* we went downstairs for *prasad*. I told Chandra to take all the materials left after *abishekam*, and bring them to her husband.

When we went upstairs, to our amazement the statue was producing *amrith* and the tray was full. I got a bottle and filled it with *amrith* to give Chandra to take to her dying husband. Then, I proceeded to lecture her on detachment. She was holding on to her husband; he could not leave his body. A doctor himself, before he went into a coma, he was aware of his deadly illness. Chandra took the *amrith* and every day gave him a few drops. Two weeks later he was able to let go of the body. Chandra thanked me for having lectured her on detachment.

Baba in a tuxedo dancing with my mom

I have had dreams throughout the years but this one in particular is very significant. It shows how Swami appeases us in times of crisis.

In 1995 my mom ended up hospitalized. I get a call from my sister-in-law who happens to be a doctor herself in Honduras. She proceeds to tell me that she thinks my mother is gravely ill. I meditated and called on Swami to do what he thinks he must do with my mom. I was very worried, but that night I had a dream that went like this:

I see Baba dressed in a black tuxedo, I see my mom dressed in a beautiful long gown. They are dancing on a marble floor. My mom looked radiant. The next day I called to find out how is my mother doing, and my sister-in-law still gives me a dire prognosis. I just told her: "Listen, my mom is fine, just get her out of that hospital." Next time I called she was out of the hospital and doing fine. In that dream Baba gave me the certainty that my mom was not yet going to die. I love Baba's *leelas* in my life.

Maurice's stay at the ashram

Once again, Baba is calling Maurice. We go to *bhajans* at the Lighthouse and an old time devotee announces that he is giving auditions to those who might want to be in a play representing the U.S. which will be performed at Sathya Sai Baba's birthday celebrations of 1996. The play was about Abraham Lincoln and Maurice ends up with the role Minister of War. Swami, gave the participants a lot of attention. I stayed in New York, but one day I got up and felt a strong feeling that Maurice should stay beyond Birthday, through Christmas. I know how beautiful and wholesome Christmas celebration is in *Prasanthi*. I told Maurice of my feeling and he agreed. His stay extended to several months. He came back deeply renewed.

VICISSITUDES

My Friend Ana, the Latin Buddhist Nun

The next year we embarked in another trip to go and visit Swami. A friend and devotee, Audre, a successful New York, actress, joined us. The three of us crossed the Atlantic. As we enter the ashram we see Lama Ana, an ordained Buddhist from Mexico. Let me give you a brief introduction to our dear friend Ana.

We had met Ana during the general assembly at the United Nations back in the 70's. At that time she was married to a very talented Mexican journalist, Luis Manuel. He spoke several languages, played classical music on the piano, was well versed in world history and his passion was to rub elbows with diplomats at the UN. He had a knack for socializing. Once we were at a cocktail at the Waldorf Astoria. Among the guests were the King of Nepal, representatives of several countries, and of course Kurt Waldheim, the secretary general. Luis Manuel tried to impress me by telling me that those dignitaries would come to greet him, and not the other way around. I laughed and told him what a big ego he had. Well, as soon as I finished telling him off, Kurt Waldheim, the secretary general comes to welcome Luis Manuel and say hello to me. That sort of life, having breakfast at the delegates lounge and attending countless diplomatic receptions night after night unfortunately aggravated his alcoholic tendencies. A few years later, Luis Manuel perished of liver disease in Mexico.

Ana, on the other hand was very intrigued with our experiences with Sai Baba. She decided to go to India for three months. She ended up in Tibet where she stayed for three years. She lived in monasteries, became an ordained nun, and wrote a book *Otro Mundo en este Mundo* (Another world within this world). My mother loved her book.

When Ana saw us arrive in *Prasanthi*, she was about to leave. She had been with the Mexican group to whom Swami had granted an interview. She decided to stay longer to be with us. In the meantime, the American group asked us to join the group. I told Audre that I prefer to be on our own. For such few days I did not want to get distracted with group energy; after all my relationship is directly with Swami.

"We all know, this is our last stop"

One day after morning *darshan*, Helen, someone that had moved to live in India started walking with me. I had introduced her to Baba in the early 70's. As we are talking on the way to the round houses, Jerry Bass is walking with his two daughters. I see that he is fragile, thin, and slow at talking. I thought he had had a mini stroke and was on his way to recovery. Helen tells me: "Don't you remember Jerry?" He looked at me and said: "Rosa, I remember you from Hilda Charlton's meetings." I tracked back to 25 years before and my memory codes recognized him. As we talked, he was holding hands with both girls. At the end of our conversation, I gave him a hug and said to him: "Don't you worry, we all know that this is our

128

last stop" and Helen and I watched him walk away till he got to his guest house. Then Helen revealed to me that Jerry was extremely sick, he had a brain tumor. I was surprised he was going to *darshans* just like everybody else.

That day I had to go to Bangalore; Air India had lost my luggage and five days after my arrival they called to let me know to go to Bangalore to pick up my lost luggage. We stayed overnight in Bangalore. The next day as soon as we arrived, the American group was looking for us to tell us that the day before, Jerry had gone up to his flat right after *darshan* and collapsed. He was taken to the hospital and he had expired. He was going to be cremated that afternoon, and we were to join the group to take Jerry's body to the Chitravati river.

I remembered the last words that I uttered when I said goodbye to Jerry. I had no idea why I had said them. I was feeling compassion for his wife and those two beautiful young girls. They would no longer have paternal love. I unpacked and got ready, wearing a white *sari* for the occasion. At 4pm I go to the library as we'd been told, but there is nobody from the American group. I waited for a long time. Suddenly, Ana, my converted Tibetan nun, comes my way. I explained to her what had happened. Would she take a rickshaw with me to go to the hospital? We went to the super specialty hospital and we were told Jerry's body had not been there, to try the old hospital. So we did! We arrived and by then we were told the whole group had taken Jerry's body to the cremation site.

We asked the rickshaw guy to please take us to the river bank and please wait for us. To our amazement when Ana and I get there, there is nobody, but the body was still burning. I said to Ana: "I thought they were going to keep singing *bhajans* throughout the cremation, how come they left him alone!" I asked Ana to please recite the Tibetan prayers for the dead which she knows by heart.

Ana was praying with her hands folded. There I was, elevating my arms and telling Jerry to go in peace and bliss, to liberate his spirit. This went on for about an hour and a half. The sun went down and it became dark. At some point the fire made a noise and there were sparkles. I realized the spirit had gone to heaven and left the body for good.

Ana and I were quiet. We got back to the ashram; as I am telling Ana: "It is a good thing I did not tell Maurice about this, because he is very sensitive," we see Maurice walking towards us with his flute in the Sai Ram bag. I tell him: "You have no idea where we have been and what we have gone through; Jerry was cremated and Ana and I were the last two people in this world to see him off." Then Maurice tells us: "Well, I was one of four people who carried the body, alongside Dr. Goldstein."

The next day, morning *darshan*, Swami called the American group for interview. Audre tells me: "Maybe we should have joined the group". I said to her: "No, I think this interview was strictly for the widow and the girls." The American devotees had given so much support to this family.

Interview on First Darshan

August 30 is my birthday. Deep in my heart I am expecting Swami to give us an interview. Before *darshan* we stopped to say hello to our dear friend Dr. Subarao, the founder of the UN Sai group, and his wife; she gave me a stainless steel container with basmati rice, which Baba could bless on such a special day. Baba came out morning and evening *darshan* but did not even look at me. I was deflated.

It just happens that Laurent, Maurice's French nephew and his girlfriend, Emily, had gone that summer to Ramana Maharshi's ashram. Laurent had met Yogi Shanti when he was eight years old, spending a holiday with us. He visited again when he was finishing his baccalaureate and he was writing his thesis on Gandhi. Somehow, our love for India was a bit contagious. Now he was in his 20's. We had suggested to Laurent to drop by and visit us in *Prasanthi*. They surprised us that day. They were not dressed for the ashram; they decided to stay in a hotel in Puttaparthi. That evening Ana invited all of us to go and have dinner at Sai

Towers to celebrate my birthday. We had not heard any news from the outside world, but that evening all the Westerners were stunned to learn Princess Diana had died in a car accident. We sent her prayers.

The next day we go to morning *darshan* and did not see our nephew. At about 11am they showed up and I told them, first and foremost they have to dress like all of us. Maurice gave a white cotton outfit to Laurent, and Emily had a long skirt, blouse and a shawl. We sat in our room. Now we were six: Ana, Audre, Laurent, Emily, Maurice and I. We are a tiny group and must be pro-active. We should go to the town and get six silk scarves made to identify our group. Should Swami approach us, what do we tell him as the name of our group?

We were brainstorming for names: *prema*?, international?, and so on. We finished our meeting, got our scarves made and went to afternoon *darshan*. Swami comes out and Audre asks for interview, with success. We all got up, but I was concerned that Emily might not have understood the procedure. I was looking for her, but when I get to the veranda I realize she was the first one to have arrived.

Again, each time Swami calls for interview I have butterflies in my stomach, my legs are shaking, I am making sure my shoulders are completely covered with a shawl. My mind is racing: "What am I going to talk to him about?" So many personal and worldly issues that I worry about. But I decided to be gracious and let everyone else express their concerns; I was to keep quiet.

Swami was so wonderful and gave a lot of attention and advice to Laurent. I could not believe that here was Laurent interacting with Swami in a private interview on his first *darshan*. How lucky! No hardship for him; look what I had gone through in the early years! It is all *karma*, no doubt.

When we come out of the inner room, I am sitting by the window. Swami asked me to pass the basket full of *vibhuti* packets. I take the bag, grabbed a bunch of packets and put them in my shawl. Baba looks at me and tells me to put them back. I implored him: "Baba, these are for my family members." I put them back, pass on the basket and he proceeded to distribute these packets to everyone. When it came to me he gave a bunch equivalent to the ones I had grabbed. I counted them and there were one for each member of my family. Baba hands me the basket again to put it back on the window sill. At that very moment, a light bulb lit up in my mind. "My God!" Today is the 31st in India but it is the 30th in the West. I was born in the West and today is my real birthday. Swami never makes a mistake; he is so precise, so detailed-oriented, so punctual, such a perfectionist. Again, we come out of the interview room, and I am floating. I am so happy for our tiny group. Swami made this trip worthwhile.

Swami is magic to me and I felt he had given me a wonderful present. He is my father and my mother. He pours so much Love to all of us. No wonder I think of him every single day of my life. I visualize millions of hearts emanating from my heart reaching his heart. I have never met any other being on this earth to be as magnificent, as extraordinary, as loving as

Sathya Sai. We are blessed to have this opportunity in this *samsara*.

Test, test, testing my faith

For about three years my doctor kept telling me I should undergo a simple procedure (laparoscopy) in order to remove an ovarian cyst. I fear any medical intervention and pray for healing. Finally on July 27, 2000, I faced the music and said to myself: "Let's get it over with." As the mask for anesthesia is placed on my face, I panic and call on Baba. "Oh God! What if I don't wake up?"

I wake up that evening and Maurice and my hematologist are by my side to give me the bad and good news. Bad because the simple laparoscopy turned into abdominal surgery. Good, the cysts were benign. Abdominal surgery is extremely painful; every few minutes I would administer morphine. For a couple of days I could not eat; I was out most of the time. On the third day as I am waking up, I see nine beings, dressed in white with a huge *mala* (strung prayer beads) around the waist, come out from the back of my bed, walk slowly and disappear, entering the wall in front of me. I said to myself: "Now I am out of any danger." I was determined to get up and start walking, even though I still had tubes of IV's. On the same floor there were lots of newly born. I went to visit them a few times a day, a true miracle of life. Some mothers with caesarean were in pain. I told them: "Keep walking, the body needs movement." Easier said than done. I myself came home, and every hour on the hour would walk around the meditation room, but the pain was persistent. I did not want to take pain killers; I wanted to heal with the least chemical intervention.

Spiritual Leaders at the UN Millennium Conference

I am struggling to recover. Luckily I have almost every single book written on Sathya Sai Baba, and innumerable *bhajan* recordings. This is my survival kit.

Yogi Shanti comes to visit the last week of August. He had fallen down a flight of stairs in Chicago and had fractured his right arm. Here is

Maurice taking care of me and now he has to take care of Yogi Shanti. He did it with so much patience and understanding.

Yogi is to attend the Millennium World Peace Summit Conference of Religious and Spiritual Leaders at the United Nations. He asks us to join him. I declined but encouraged Maurice to attend, this was an important event. Spiritual leaders from different parts of the world had come to New York to participate in this event.

Could Baba visit the UN?

In fact, a few years before I had had this dream:

Swami's devotees, dressed in white, were gathered around the fountain at the main entrance of the UN building. Dignitaries were coming in alongside. Sai Baba was blessing by sprinkling drops of water on our heads. I was carrying a little bucket with the holy water and walking by his side. When I was running out of water I would call a devotee to replenish it.

We always thought that if Baba addressed the General Assembly he could transform the hearts and minds of world leaders who need spiritual understanding in order to vote on policies that can bring peace and prosperity for all in this world.

Prior to this Conference, the only spiritual leader to address the world body had been the Pope, as a representative of the Vatican State. Perhaps, we thought, this event would serve as a precedent to an actual visit by Sathya Sai Baba.

Birthday at the Waldorf

The second day of the Conference coincided with my birthday, August 30. Both Yogi and Maurice convinced me to join them.

What a surprise! The ballroom at the Waldorf Astoria was full of spiritual leaders. At lunch, I was assigned to a table with nine *sadhus* from India, naturally, all dressed in orange. These were Sanskrit scholars. I felt this was a direct gift from Baba to me. There were 108 *sadhus* from India; there were some Chinese dressed in national gowns, a couple of Quechua Indians from Peru. There was the president of the

University of Peace in Costa Rica and many other high ranking people.

Guess what! Ted Turner, founder of CNN, was there as a keynote speaker; he was also picking up the tab for this conference. I would normally see him in events like this at the ballroom of the Waldorf or other hotels for broadcasting events. He recognized me because 25 years ago when he had arrived from Cuba and gave a very heated talk in one of those luncheons, I approached him, and he asked me if I was Cuban; I said no, I was born in Honduras. He immediately smiled and told me he loved sailing in Roatan. This is a beautiful island in the north coast of Honduras. According to sailing magazine it is one of the three most beautiful and safest places in the world to scuba dive. We shared our love for Roatan and the business of television. I had the opportunity to talk to Ted and he told me how much he hates poverty. We all have to work hard to eradicate hunger and poverty in this world.

The conference went on for an entire week. The themes were very interesting. I attended some of the controversial ones, i.e. Hindus and Moslems. In this particular session a Moslem leader takes the podium and starts his discourse by pointing out how peaceful they are. A young Hindu *sadhu* takes a microphone in the audience and goes ballistic. I had to intervene by scolding the Hindu *sadhu*. Even security at the hotel had to show up. Oh God! Why don't we learn to just love and understand one another on earth? If religious leaders behave like this, what can we expect from the masses?

Anyhow, that evening we were invited to dinner by the Hindu delegates at a temple in New Jersey. The decorations were festive; there were a few discourses followed by sumptuous dinner. What a special birthday I had! I felt this was a gift from Swami.

The conference was full of peace-seeking people. The Waldorf Astoria lobby was a spectacle to behold. There were *sadhus* sitting on the floor, some were lying down, some were repeating mantras, just like they do in their holy places in India.

In the meantime, our dear friend Yogi Shanti was having the time of his life. Imagine! He had a cast in his arm in a position as if he was blessing people. There were a group of beautiful young women from the Endeavor Academy, dedicated to a Course in Miracles. They would sit around Yogi and massage his back, his legs, his arms. They pampered him and he blessed them and told them interesting stories from the Ramayana.

At the end of the conference Yogi invited several spiritual leaders from different religions to come and have a meeting in our meditation room. It was a convenient place. I was stunned! Imagine! These were very special people and here they were in our own place visiting us!

Later on, Yogi invited the young women from Endeavor Academy to come early evening. Oh my God! They came to give a presentation, but I saw they were unprepared. They went into our office to make long distance calls, even to India. I was highly insulted when they made mockery of my altar and Baba's picture, to the point that they would not stay in the meditation room.

After that experience I prayed to Baba to please send only those that he wants to have visit him, not intruders.

Our week-long attendance at the Conference had a healing effect on me. I started walking normally and regaining strength after the surgery. Yogi Shanti's presence was comic relief. He had a tremendous sense of humor. At the same time, his presence provided an ashram-like atmosphere.

Bad Publicity on Sathya Sai

One day I come back from work and find Maurice sitting down and looking really sad. A Sai devotee had called him and urged him to go to the Indian store to buy the magazine *India Today*

This issue had a cover story about Swami, his seventy-fifth birthday celebrations, his materializations, etc. The issue also included an article that had the most severe accusations. As I finished reading the article I just said to Maurice: "This holds no water. Swami is our friend. We have seen him throughout the years just give, give and give non-stop to all people. I have seen him feed the poor, one by one and talk sweetly to them. We, ourselves have been recipients of his love and generosity. I do not believe one word about this article. *Rakshasas* want to discredit my holy teacher. How sick can they be?" In the aftermath we kept learning that some of the 'holier than thou' devotees were dropping out like flies. Not me, not Maurice. I said: "The whole world can be against Swami but not me. I know who he is. I have seen him heal people even at a distance. He has showered our lives with *Leelas*. We are just deeply grateful to Swami."

We had met the naysayers and had intuitively kept a distance. One of the ill doers, from Sweden, in the past gave a talk in New York. I listened to him and as soon as he finished I left. I disliked him, I did not feel any attraction to go and greet him. Now, years later, I realized that my intuition was right on. Also, there was a well known English pianist; we were called to see if we could put him up for a few days. Maurice was inclined to offer him Baba's room, but I said: "If he is well known why doesn't he

144

stay with those who are his fans?" I went up to Baba's room, prayed and asked him to please bring to our place only those whom he thinks we should receive. The next day we got a call telling us that some other people had welcomed the pianist. I was relieved. Swami says that it is very important to be in the company of good people. To my amazement, this character was instrumental in defaming Swami. Again, my intuition proved to be correct.

Newcomers to the Ashram

Having had a medical intervention in 2000 and having come out of surgery with flying colors, plus the incredible experience during recovery, I made my priority to go and thank Swami and pay respect.

My friend Claudine from France joined us. Claudine had had a severe accident a few years before and had a metal insert in her leg. I thought that for sure she was going to sit with the sick people who get chairs. To my amazement, Claudine decided to sit on the marble floor like everybody else. I took her to Dr. Rao's for *ayurvedic* massage. She adapted

145

beautifully to the routine of the ashram. The first day she put on a *sari* she wrapped it on the opposite side. As we were walking to *darshan*, all the Indian ladies were laughing at her. Here is a woman who is a French designer of Haute Couture! She loved the prints in silk *saris*. She mastered the art of wrapping eight yards of material and of course she was wearing "Christian Dior" sandals, unlike the rest of us who buy simple flipflops.

I had also invited my Argentine friend Raquel, a flight attendant to join us and experience Swami's *darshan*, but her schedule did not allow a lengthy stay. That day, Claudine and I are at Dr. Rao's for our *ayurvedic* massage. I go to reception and there is Raquel with her sunglasses, waiting for us. Somehow, she managed to fly from San Francisco, New York, Paris, Bombay, Bangalore, then take a taxi to Puttaparthi. We went to accommodations and requested a room to be shared by Claudine and Raquel.

Raquel was in cultural shock but managed. During *darshan*, as we all know, the sense of personal space that Westerners have is big in comparison to Indians. Raquel used to get so annoyed when some Indian ladies would simply accommodate themselves by resting their elbows on her back. I have no idea why they would do that to Raquel, it never happened to me.

We formed a small group with the Bailey sisters, with whom we were seeking the opportunity to sing for Baba. During that trip Baba did not call on us. He gave several interviews to people from Iran, and another American group were blessed with several interviews.

Devastating Experience for New Yorkers

At work, we had a sales meeting at 8am. One of the presidents is talking and realizes that he needs to go into his office to pick up a file. Upon his return he announces that a plane just crashed into the World Trade Center. I said: "Are you kidding?" He says: "no." I got up, went to my own area and turned on the TV; others followed me. We saw the damage the first plane had caused. I immediately said: "This is terrorism big time!" My co-workers said: "Come on, Rosa, you are crazy." I started praying and imagining what those people inside that building were going through, when all of a sudden we see the second plane is going to hit the other building. I started thinking of people I knew who worked at the World Trade Center. Still, people in the office thought it was a control tower error. I kept telling them, "Do you think the pilots are blind?" It was a crystal clear day in September. I was convinced that New York had been attacked by terrorists.

Then the third plane accident in Pittsburgh, plus the uncertainty of a possible attack on the United Nations and the White House. I called Maurice; we happen to live in Tudor City across from the UN. He turned on the TV, saw what happened and turned it off. He finished his morning meditation. But of course, we all got swept up in the ensuing live coverage of this apocalyptic event.

The whole world knows how deep an injury this event has been for the U.S. and the entire planet. Life changed after 9/11. Our friends,

even children, called us, from France, from
Honduras, from all over the world. People
whom we had not heard from in years were
asking how we were. We volunteered to do
seva, we attended religious acts; people were
frantic and paranoid. On top of it all, there came
the anthrax scare. In a building in our
neighborhood men dressed for a lunar landing
went in to respond to an anthrax call, just to
realize someone going into the laundry room
had a bit of laundry detergent fall out of the
box.

Two days after the Towers event, Raquel,
Maurice and I went to Central Park for respite.
It was a crystal clear day. We contemplated
nature and walked and walked through intricate
parts of the park. On 72nd street there was a
group of musicians playing jazz. It was such a
melancholic sound, they were playing from
their hearts; clearly it was dedicated to the
victims. But life was back, parents strolling
with their children who bicycled, ran, had tiny
boats in the basin and had snacks. Yes! Life is
beautiful, people are precious and New York is
a stupendous city. It adopted me, and I love it

and pray for its safety. In New York, 150 languages are spoken every day, people of all ethnic backgrounds, all religions, come together in this unique place. Why in the world would anyone want to destroy New York? I was outraged, with indignation at such malice. At the end of the day, familiar with the smell of cremation, I recognized this smell even in uptown Manhattan. I repeated the *Gayatri Mantra* non-stop. I kept my prayers for those who were totally surprised, who had no time perhaps to call on God before leaving the planet.

A few days after the tragedy, Yogi Shanti came and persuaded us to go down to the site in Battery Park City to meditate for the souls of those who had perished. As soon as I saw the devastation, a deep pain hit my heart; a knot in my throat would not allow me to utter a single word. I could not stop sobbing. I had never in my life felt such pain, anguish and disbelief that human beings could cause so much damage. Yogi's company was a blessing; we went home and had our own ritual for the victims of 9/11.

Because we had come back from *Prasanthi* a week prior to this horrific act, I was relatively calm. I always hold on to our survival kit, Swami's teachings, always remembering:

"Do not fear that I am here."

But the reality for most new Yorkers was different. One could see the fear in their faces, but it also brought out the best in people. A lot of generosity, a lot of prayers, people opened up. Two would start talking while riding a bus and all of a sudden eight others would join the conversation.

Nonetheless, the New York police was working non-stop. The sirens in the neighborhood would not stop day or night. The entire neighborhood had been closed because of the UN. There were tractors and hundreds of police cars. We had to show our ID's even to get back into our own neighborhood. During the night, sirens would not allow us to sleep. Maurice got depressed and lost 20 pounds.

By Thanksgiving we were at the end of our rope. We decided to go to Honduras to the

Copan Ruins, a Mayan archeological site. At least we knew of a place that would be quiet. For the first time in months we had a full night's sleep. Copan Ruins is a clear example that the Mayans had spiritual wisdom. The topography and weather of that place make it an ideal contemplative retreat. We also visited family and friends in Tegucigalpa. After a short sojourn we recovered and got back to New York. The war-like trucks were still in front of the UN.

Hosting UN Sai group

During this chaotic time, high security at the UN did not allow groups to meet in the building.

We again offered the UN group to come and hold meetings every Friday in our apartment. Baba had sent this group for the second time. Such *satsang* is especially important in times of crisis.

Special Experiences awaiting in 2002

In using my yearly vacation time, we had decided to go one year to Swami and one year to see my mom. Every time I would ask my mother, should I go to Swami or to her; most of the time she would say "go to Baba, it does a lot of good to you both." Christmas 2001, after having gone through the horrific experience in NY, we decided to go to *Prasanthi*. Christmas is a special time for Westerners and Baba gives a lot of attention.

By Easter of the following year, I told my mom that I felt a strong pull to come and visit her. Immediately she said: "Yes come!" We arrived and my mom was bedridden with rheumatoid arthritis. In one interview I had told Swami about my concern for her in old age. He said to me that she was going to have her mental faculties till the end of her life, and so it was.

Her mind was a very accurate computer. She knew everybody's telephone number by heart. She was the moral coach to the grandchildren, relatives and friends. She was very charismatic. Every day she had people visit her and she made sure there was food for everyone.

During the first five days of visiting Nila, my mother, we talked about everything; I was her confidant. Sonia, my cousin visited; she has a caustic sense of humor with a political slant. My mother, who listened to world news and was up to date with politics, would not miss a beat. We laughed a lot.

Maurice would sit with my mom and discuss religion. As she had strong resistance to a prophet from India, he would read from the Bible and *A Course in Miracles* in Spanish. She enjoyed these sessions, which complemented the spiritual nurturing she received from her Evangelist circle of friends. That particular day she noticed she had low blood pressure. Because she was more prone to high blood pressure that as far as I know can cause strokes, I did not get alarmed, but told her I would call the doctor. My sister in law who is also a doctor took her blood pressure and was not alarmed either.

That evening we talked. I had brought her a new set of bed covers; I was trying to convince her to allow me to paint the bedroom. She said:

"You are on vacation, come for a few days, and all you do is clean up my closets and take care of things here."

The next morning, I go out for my early morning walk. The maid comes out and starts calling me, she was crying. Immediately I knew something serious had happened to my mom, but never imagined how serious. When I came into the room, my stepfather, my youngest brother and his wife, and helpers were in the room. I saw she had left her body. I took a pocket of *vibhuti* and spread it on her now lifeless body. Marlene, her Evangelist friend arrived a few moments later. She is a nurse and a generous soul. She helps poor people, children with cancer, children without parents, and so on. Marlene proceeded to dress the body for funeral rites.

My stepfather and brothers went to make arrangements at a funeral home. I went to the flower shop and bought the entire shop to ornament the church. The wake was to take place at the Evangelist church she had belonged to. In Honduras, you also feed friends and family who keep you company in these times. My sister-in-law and I went to the supermarket to buy food. We gathered the maids from three houses to help with the cooking.

I decided to extend my stay for another five days in order to wrap up practical affairs. I collected mom's belongings, made a list of relatives and friends and assigned something special to each one of them. I only kept a shawl. At critical times, I have a lot of endurance. I am a practical person but I kept on calling God to help me go through these very difficult days. Crying and becoming helpless does not help those around.

Baba's visiting card gives me comfort

The biggest loss we can have is losing one's mother. That unconditional love is gone forever. So many years have gone by and I still miss calling my mom. I found strength by resuming my work responsibilities. Nonetheless, I was walking around with a knot in my throat upon my return to New York. Three weeks after our return to New York, my friend Simi called asking for company to buy jewelry for her daughter's upcoming wedding. I said to her: "Simi, it is a very rainy Saturday, I am not the happy-go-lucky person that you know. I am still feeling the sudden departure of my mom." Simi insisted that I go with her because she was carrying substantial cash and was driving alone to Edison, New Jersey. She was persuasive and I agreed to spend the day with her.

That day, my mother's presence was intense. I thought of all the favorite things she enjoyed in this life. She loved flowers, theater, music, philosophy, religion, the colors lila and aqua. She loved nature, animals, but above all she loved her children. She was in constant communication with all of us. She always advised me to be more prudent, but she admired the fact that I do not lie. I am straight as an arrow. In some ways, I acted like her mother. I bought all her clothing, cosmetics and medications; I enjoyed buying trinkets for her. Whenever I bought something for myself, I felt compelled to offer her something as well.

That rainy Saturday was long and tedious. Simi took hours to choose the jewelry; I just wanted to come home to my meditation room. But the outing was going to be extended by stopping off at her in-laws who invited us for dinner. It continued to pour and we waited to see if the rain let up.

Veena plays by itself

What a long day. Finally by 11pm I get home. Maurice is already sleeping. While I am climbing the stairway I feel butterflies in my stomach; I was feeling something that I cannot explain. I turn on the lights, I hear a sound and realize the *veena* in the corner of the room is playing by itself. "Am I going crazy, listening to sounds where there is no radio or cassette recording?" I step out of the room into the foyer and I still hear the music. I remembered that when Sai Baba was born a *tamboura* played by itself. I went back into the room; the strings of the *veena* are moving and producing the melodious sound. I immediately sit in front of Swami's picture and - lo and behold! - *vibhuthi* materializes in the entire picture. I sat there in awe and realize Baba is blessing us with a visiting card. It must have been 3am when I decided to go to sleep.

Sunday morning I tell Maurice to come into the meditation room because we have to sit and meditate together, contemplating this *leela*. After meditation he lies down on the couch, starts humming a few *bhajans* and suddenly we see that a picture he placed in another corner of the room is being covered with *vibhuti* as well.

That special day we stayed quiet, did not talk to anyone. I have seen that devotees flock to places where phenomena occur and I still felt fragile and tired, I was in mourning. But after this extraordinary experience, I no longer felt a knot in my throat, my heart lightened up, my mind was reassured that my mom is in peace and bliss. I can only be happy for her and grateful for having been instrumental in giving me life. Baba healed my sorrow.

No one knew about Swami's visiting card. I was planning to call close friends to help me set up a special *bhajan* for this occasion, but on Monday morning Maurice gets a call from two devotees from Connecticut – they are coming to New York to pick up their Indian visas for their forthcoming trip. They are among the first people to experience this visiting card. Only Baba knows whom he brings and when. I consider this meditation room his mini-*mandir*.

Actually, in one interview I had the audacity to ask him: "Swami, if you ever come to New York, would you stay with us?" He laughed and responded: "I am already there with you, always with you." I was fantasizing that if Swami ever came, devotees could gather downstairs and he would grant interviews upstairs.

Ending career 2005

A difficult year. Spring in Paris for ten days to visit our relatives was a much needed break from the stressful job I had. Five minutes before leaving we get a call from India to let us know that our dear friend Yogi Shanti decided to leave his body during the performance of a *yagna*.

Yogi had sent us the most beautiful invitation card for attendance to that particular event, which would be a milestone of his spiritual career. He also called practically every morning between 7 and 8am. At times I could hardly say hello to him for I was rushing off to work. The year before we had met Sai Ma at the Windham Retreat upstate New York, where two Sai devotees host various new-age groups and workshops. Somehow we had connected Sai Ma with Yogi Shanti, and he invited her as a special guest to be part of the *yagna*. In fact Yogi's last call from Haridwar was riding in a car with Sai Ma.

The idea that I would never again see Yogi Shanti overwhelmed me. I cried the entire flight New York to Paris.

When we got back from Paris, Maurice took a one-week intensive with Sai Ma and her group. It was during this week that I lose my job of nearly 28 years in the most unexpected way. The company was to be sold and they were cutting back. I was never given any warning, I was in shock!

As a pragmatic person, I dealt with whatever I had to deal with in terms of legalities. But the stress of legal battles took a toll on both Maurice and me.

By December all we wanted was to go and see Swami. In prior years in an interview I had told him: "Baba, I don't want to have any bosses. I only want you as my boss" He responded: "You stay there, make some money." Every time I felt frustrated at work, I remembered Swami's advice. In the years I was there, the company I worked for grew more than tenfold and was sold three times. I was able to realize the American dream of advancement by merit, but now the new management was ruthless. To regain our health and mental equanimity, we spent the Winter in Prasanthi Nilayam.

Shivarathri Lingam

Spending the night of *Shivarathri* in the ashram is an impactful experience, but especially so when a *lingam* issues forth from the mouth of the Avatar. Everyone wants to see this happen, at least once in a lifetime, in spite of often unruly crowd behavior. I was privileged to

162

witness the creation of two golden *lingam*s, one materialized with the wave of his hand, the other produced from his body, almost popping out of his mouth, bouncing twice on the table, and swiftly caught with his hand. It is said that having experienced such an event relieves one of the necessity to re-incarnate. At the very least, in this lifetime, it is a deeply healing miraculous gift.

God Lives in India

April Bailey, a very talented Sai devotee, has been writing songs dedicated to Swami for many years. Audrey, her sister, with a melodious jazz background, put together an accompanying choir group of which Maurice and I have been part of since its inception. After ten years effort, a CD was complete *God Lives in India*, and the group was being considered for performance at *Prasanthi*. While I was in the ashram, every other week I would walk into the administrator's office with the same request: "Can the Bailey sisters group be invited for *Guru Purnima*?" By chance, when we are about to leave he tells me that we should be contacting a coordinator in Argentina if we were interested in participating in the event. Back in the US, I transmitted this to Audrey.

We continue to rehearse, until one day news comes that we are invited; off we went to India through Kuala Lumpur in Malaysia.

Oh God! It was so hard to believe this small group was in front of Baba. My two alto partners could not make it and it's as if I am all alone in front of Baba. I always tell people. "Only Baba can make a frog sing." There is a DVD *God Lives in India* as a documentary of this wonderful event of 2006. I was amazed how self-confident I felt in front of the Avatar. These songs are in English and we were wondering how Indian devotees would react. It was awesome! When we finished, Indian ladies would come to embrace us with tears in their eyes. They loved the performance and told us our singing was heartfelt. Baba's *leela*!

Ati Rudra Maha Yagna

Maurice and I were to leave early August. Suddenly, I started hearing about this extraordinary event that was to take place dedicated to Lord *Shiva* and in thousands of years had not been performed and its purpose was to benefit humanity, for the spiritual health of the whole world. We could not find any information other than hearsay about the event but two old-time devotees emphatically told me it was imperative for me to stay – this was a once in a lifetime opportunity. We tried to change our tickets but the airline could not fulfill the request. We went to Bangalore, relaxed at the Lila Hotel, called once again the travel agency just to get a negative response. We were to leave at 9pm. At 5pm I felt such a strong pull to go back to *Prasanthi*; I went to the airport with Maurice but got cold feet; I simply had to attend this special event that had to do with Lord *Shiva*. I was torn, how could I leave Maurice alone in the last minute? That is out of character for me. Baba's call was so strong. I had to go back, so I did!

I did not miss a minute of twelve days of the rituals of the *Yagna*. At 3am I was up and ready to imbibe this incredible energy created by Swami and 132 priests with *vedic* chanting non-stop and performing synchronized rituals on 11 *homas*. The setting was spectacular, the hypnotic chanting of the priests made me go beyond the body into a blissful experience! Swami's love made me come back and bathe in that aura of peace. My unexpected attendance at this extraordinary event is another of Swami's *leelas* in my life. I am grateful!

Searching for a slice of Paradise 2007

Maurice loves the sea, so do I but he knows sailing and wind surfing. So, we went to Costa Rica for a ten day seminar for retirees from abroad. Then we went to Honduras, rented a four wheel drive and got into every nook and cranny of the country.

We were searching for a retirement place by the sea. We also went to the mountains, the valleys and the area of the ancient Mayans.

Upon our return, my sister in law called telling us they had been invited to Palma Real, where she thought it could be the place for us. This is a gated community where the hotel had extended to building villas. Just by looking on the internet we made a decision to buy a villa. The price was right and it offered sea and mountains, right in front of Cayos Cochinos where they film Survivor for Italy and Spain. A month after we decided to buy we went to spend the winter. Now we would have a place where to escape from the cold, a luxury but a medical imperative for my condition of hemolytic anemia, which is aggravated with exposure to cold weather.

MIRACLE

Encountering Death

Waking up, I realized I was in a space capsule. Why? Had I just come back from other planets? I think I was in Iraq in a bomb blast, and it hit my head. What happened? I just had my head sawed open by a surgeon and his team that apparently saved my life. I was floating in space. Oh yes! I had just come back from a very peaceful place where this very attractive light was guiding the path. I realized something serious had happened to the physical body and I said: "I want to go. It is so peaceful here. I don't want to live with a decrepit body in a chaotic world." But suddenly, I was dressed in a beautiful long gown, beige and pink, and started turning like a spinning top, or ballet ballerina. The light and a strong wind were pushing me back into this world. At that point I realized my *karma* was not yet finished. That was my mini-mystical encounter with death.

What a conundrum! (hematology)

Let me tell you what happened to me. In the year 2000 I was diagnosed with hemolytic anemia. My hemoglobin was at a 7.5; normal range is 12. What caused this type of anemia? The hematologist told me that it was inherited from European royalty. I laughed and said: "Very nice, they left me the blue blood but not the castle." I was given iron supplements. Being a health freak, I also ate any food containing iron. But in 2008, another hematologist found that in addition to the anemia, I had developed too much iron in the blood, a more serious condition, which can affect other organs of the body. What a conundrum: too little iron, too much iron! The proposed treatment for iron overload was weekly blood-letting (phlebotomies), the equivalent of donating half a liter of blood on a weekly basis for a year or more! The problem is that this process would aggravate the anemia. To address the anemia, a form of chemotherapy that required hospitalization was proposed. I was reluctant and fearful to undergo such treatments. What did I do?

Swami gives padnamaskar (touching holy feet) to my heart

I decided that first I would go to see Sathya Sai Baba, my guru. Arriving in *Prasanthi Nilayam* (Abode of Peace) to me is like going home. The highlight of the trip was in *Darshan* (Seeing a Holy Being). I was in front row. Sai Baba was approaching with his wheelchair, but he was coming directly at me, very fast, and I got scared. It looked as if he was going to run me over. The *shakti* (energy) that I felt was so strong that all I could do was to cry out loud saying: "Baba, Baba, Babaaaa!" But then we both started laughing like kids. The amazing thing is how young he looked, just like the picture of him as a young man upon which I had meditated for 30 years. My heart was beating so fast that it felt as if it had jumped out of my chest, bounced two or three times on the marble floor, with a final jump onto Swami's feet.

I felt such a relief to get *Padnamaskar* (Touching the Feet of a Holy Being), even in such a dramatic fashion. Only Swami knows when and how to bless us. When *Darshan* was over, some of the Indian ladies witnessing this episode came to touch me, having witnessed such intense interaction between Baba and a devotee.

Back to the West

My companion and caregiver throughout this adventure is my husband, Maurice. We arrived in New York on Halloween. I underwent the four chemo treatments during November. Because my type of anemia is aggravated by cold, my doctors had advised me to avoid New York winters if possible. So in December we went to our paradise on the north coast of Honduras with the intention to spend the winter. While still in New York, however, I had been complaining to doctors of acute pain in my neck and shoulders. I was told it could be osteoarthritis, and was given pain management treatment, but no one had picked up on a neurological condition taking hold of me. In addition to the pain, I was getting weaker day by day, and more and more disoriented and forgetful, which was odd for someone like me with a type A, dynamic personality.

Honduras diagnosis

The real drama now begins to unfold, but my memory goes blank for the next month.

Apparently, in addition to the other symptoms, I was rapidly losing motor co-ordination; I began walking like a penguin. Because of the excruciating neck pain, several doctors were consulted, but it was not until January, when I was taken in emergency to D'Antoni Hospital in La Ceiba, Honduras, a small coastal city, that a young internist, Dr. Enry Melgar, immediately identified a neurological problem. Two hours later MRI results showed a brain tumor the size of a lemon. I was placed immediately in intensive care with anti-inflammatories. Dr.

Fernando Sierra, the neurosurgeon was ready to perform surgery in four days for this extremely critical condition. An invisible enemy had taken over and was threatening my life.

The Crucifixion: Surgery

The diagnosis was unequivocal. Since our insurance was valid only in the United States, I was taken by air ambulance to Miami. The surgery took place at the Jackson Memorial Hospital on January 6, 2009. I was oblivious. Baba spared me the ordeal of making the most crucial medical decision of my life. Without an immediate operation I would have gone into a coma. Divine intervention made a timely operation possible. I am sure Baba choreographed the whole thing.

Alive Again

When I came out of intensive care after brain surgery, my first reaction was: "What happened? I did not authorize to have my skull cracked!" I was furious. I never would have allowed this drastic medical intervention to take place. Maurice and the doctors in Honduras had explained everything to me but my mind had not registered; on the contrary, as an extrovert, I was joking with the medical staff, even inviting them to go to India with me to learn *ayurvedic* (traditional Indian medicine) healing.

Now when the doctors walked into my room, I thanked them but I was not grateful. I was angry, telling them: "Very nice, you saved my life but now I look like a monster!" The inflammation had deformed my face and I could not conceive of it getting back to normal. I felt like a casualty from a war zone.

I wanted them to protect my skull with jade and gold just like the Mayan skulls. The Mayans in Honduras performed skull surgery centuries ago. Another day, I visualized placing the image of the Hindu goddess of wisdom, *Saraswati*, where my surgery had taken place. At least I was brainstorming, but still, I wondered why life was so unfair. I had just begun to enjoy my retirement after a lifetime of working and this happens!

Maurice had gotten a half dozen books about the brain and done extensive internet searches. Trying my best to comprehend the severity of this intervention, during the wee hours of the night I would write my laundry list of questions for doctor's 7am visit and then say, "Here is your laundry list." He would smile "Yes, I know. I am your laundry man."

Recovery

The recovery process was very painful. In such a state of shock, I could barely sleep. Every three hours I would get injections in my stomach and arms, while my fingers were poked for blood samples. I was under intense medication, but I wanted my brain to return to normal. You can imagine how frightening it can be to regain consciousness and realize that one can't talk, can't walk, to suspect one may have a useless body for the rest of one's life. At times like these I remembered the teachings. "You are not the body; you are not the emotions; you are not the intellect; you are something Divine; you are something Supreme".

Physical Rehabilitation

It never occurred to me that walking is also a function of the brain. Nine days after surgery, I began rehabilitation. Was I now a paraplegic with little hope for recovery? What was most painful was seeing so many young people incapacitated by automobile and motorcycle accidents. Particularly impactful, was a beautiful Cuban-American woman who could only communicate by moving her eyes. The majority of these patients were in pain with full body braces like Christopher Reeves, the superman star.

My panic was such that when they brought me a wheelchair, I said to the nurse: "Take it away, I don't want to see a wheelchair in my room. I am going to walk again." I was shaky, my legs were weak, and all my muscles flabby. To help me stand up, they sent a strong and gentle Iraq war veteran who encouraged me to move my legs and march like a soldier.

I began my daily four-hour rehabilitation sessions with the enthusiasm of a marathon runner. There were all kinds of incredible

175

gadgets, but it was the therapists that helped me the most. Also there were nurses from at least 30 countries. Truly, the whole world helped me to survive this crisis. The Haitians especially had something that touched me deeply. My body ached all over, but I pushed myself. The therapist would say: "Relax, relax". I would respond: "How can I relax if I cannot walk? Push me more because I need to walk!"

Over the years since my 20's I had been doing yoga, modern dance, Middle Eastern dance, and swimming. The physical therapist was amazed at my advancement, every day I could do a bit more. She told me my body was banking on all the years I had been health-oriented. I practiced a yogic exercise: "Cosmic energy invigorates me, rejuvenates me, reverberates me" lifting your arms and hands above the head, bringing them down to your body and feeling the power of your own energy with hands in front of the solar plexus. At all times, I called on Divine intervention.

After 10 days of intense rehab, I could walk, but not independently; I did not yet have balance.

My strategy was not to use a walker or a cane, I would only hold on to another human being.

Swami's divine play

Over the years that I have meditated and asked Swami to help me open up my heart and fill it with love, I never asked him to open my skull! Needless to say, during this ordeal my relationship with Sai was a roller coaster ride. To appease myself, I did *pranayama* (breathing exercises), I repeated the *Gayatri mantra* (sacred prayer), I called on Baba constantly. My talismans included *Shiva Lingam* earrings and a locket, both materialized by Swami. The locket has the image of Sai Baba on one side and Shirdi Baba on the other side. Most people noticed it, and the typical question was: "Is that your boyfriend?" My response would be "he is my spiritual teacher." At times I would go into a more lengthy explanation.

"God lives in India," is a DVD of a *Guru Purnima* (holiday honoring the guru) 2006 performance to Sathya Sai Baba, consisting of original songs by the Bailey sisters, in which I had the honor to participate. In the hospital

177

room, this played non-stop, together with *bhajans* (devotional songs); it was my altar. Everyone who entered my room told me it was the most peaceful on the floor.

Nevertheless, sometimes I felt that Swami had abandoned me, although his presence would manifest in subtle ways. From the very beginning, I was given a VIP suite, due to a loyal ex-colleague's involvement with the hospital's foundation. In fact, as I entered the room, a long documentary about India was playing on the television. I also received an overnight package from a Sai devotee with *lingam* (holy) water and *vibhuti* (holy ash), which I consumed really fast.

Still, three weeks into this ordeal, I longed for a more dramatic sign from Baba. In the past he had blessed me with dreams, even *vibhuti* and *amrith* (divine nectar). Now, somewhere between my waking and sleeping state, I saw Baba in his wheelchair giving instructions on his left side to four Hindu priests performing a *puja* (ritual of worship). I could see the flames, the flowers, rice, clearly performing *abishekam* (ritual bathing of deity), reminding me of the twelve day *Ati Rudra Maha Yajnam* (sacred ritual) of 2006 of which I had not missed a minute. On his right side there were four angels. Baba was instructing them to help me recover. This was a much longed-for and deeply inspiring vision. Still, the drama unfolds......

Devastating

I was still under heavy anti-inflammatory and anti-seizure medications, (thanks to Baba I never suffered from headaches nor seizures, before or after surgery). The side effects of these medications played havoc with my emotions. The tumor was removed, but was it benign or malignant? At first we were told it was benign. We told family and friends and everyone was happy. Subsequently, the neurosurgeon himself explained that although officially malignant, the tumor was 99% benign, and completely removed. Upon discharge from rehabilitation, however, Maurice insisted on getting a final appointment with the hospital's Director of Neurosurgery. It is here that it finally dawned on me, a three-piece suit guy telling me that the tumor was malignant and I must follow up with chemotherapy and radiation; basically he is giving me a death sentence. My emotions at this point are like a turbulent hurricane, impossible to describe.

We met with the Director of Oncology, and he proceeds to explain the procedures for the treatment I must undertake. He actually instills fear in me by implying that not undertaking this treatment, the tumor could re-appear and at that point I would have to undergo another surgery. I said: "I'd rather die than have my skull cracked again." I was doing deep breathing to appear composed, which annoyed him to the point of his saying: "Young lady, you are going to hyperventilate and drop on my floor!" He told us the treatments should start immediately and continue for six weeks. Furthermore, it would be the wife of the corporate-looking doctor who would supervise chemotherapy, the aspect of this treatment I most dreaded. "No way!" I said, "If I'm to undergo these treatments, I'll do it in New York where we have a nice place and all my toys. It seems I'm not only a patient, but clearly a client!" He replied: "It is your pleasure!"

Back To Honduras

A crucial decision had to be made. My body, my brain and my emotions were depleted. My caregiver was exhausted. New York was in the midst of winter, not good for my anemia. We decided to postpone any further treatments, and return to our slice of paradise in Honduras for rest and recuperation.

My sister, Leslie, had flown with us to Honduras, providing invaluable companionship. She has her own Montessori school and is by nature very patient, putting up with my emotional turmoil. A severe side effect of the anti-inflammatory medication was anxiety. I took one anti-anxiety pill and hated the way it made me feel. I never took another. I wanted to control these emotions through meditation, relaxation exercises, visualizations, all the tools I had experimented with throughout the years.

As soon as we arrived in Honduras, I visited my doctors who had diagnosed the brain tumor. I wanted to embrace them and tell them how grateful I was. They reassured me that I did not need chemotherapy, but advised me to follow up with radiation as a precaution. I was comforted by their human warmth. Palma Real, a gated community surrounded by sea and mountains became my healing sanctuary.

I was doing my exercises in a disciplined manner. Walking on the sand by the sea at sunrise helped me to regain my balance and walk again on my own. Early morning the sky is like the *Mandir* (temple) in *Prasanthi Nilayam* (abode of peace) - light blue with pink and clear light - awesome! The oxygen intake while doing breathing exercises was energizing. This made me stronger day by day. Prior to this I always needed the company of someone else; I still feared I could fall. It is so wonderful to regain confidence in walking again. Towards the end, I did one kilometer every morning.

I am so grateful to mother earth, family and friends and my dear Sai brothers and sisters who included me in the prayer network. You see, prayers work! Every day of my life now, I thank Baba. I consider myself SWAMI'S WALKING MIRACLE.

New York: Beams of photons

In New York, I have to face the music. To my relief, the neuro-oncologist tells me that chemotherapy is unnecessary, and that it would have been counterproductive to start radiation immediately after surgery. But now I am part of the decision process in my treatment. Radiation is challenging. It sends photons to the tumor area to make sure no malignant cells survive. Maurice calls it a pre-emptive strike. It is war, with collateral damage – innocent cells will also perish. The alternative is the 'wait and see' approach, taking periodic MRI's, perhaps with complementary new-age modalities.

Already with a fragile short-term memory, further intervention concerns me. I forget things like putting out the candle after meditation, turning off the stove after cooking, going to the market having forgotten my wallet. Whenever I go crazy looking for something I repeat "*Om Gam Ganapathaye Namah,*" and incredibly, *Ganesh* (Hindu deity) removes obstacles and I

183

find things. We need Divine Intervention, even in the smallest details.

Having been through the crucifixion, one thing for sure, I do not fear death. I fear losing my mental capacity, becoming a burden to others, and a lack of quality of life. After second and third opinion consultations, the top Oncologist at both Weill-Cornell and Columbia Presbyterian re-assures me that after radiation, the tumor will not come back and that I'm good "for the next forty years." I bite the bullet and accept treatment.

Under radiation, facing an enormous linear accelerator, I mistrusted the competence of the technicians, the kinks with the machine; all I have left is to call on Baba. I visualize the beautiful sunrise in the Caribbean. I place Baba's image in the heart of technicians, nurses and doctors that are working on my case. Soon it will be over and done. Guess What! Just to re-assure me, Baba sent a new technician and she is a Shirdi Baba devotee. When I show up for my MRI, conversation with the receptionist reveals that her parents have a Sai Baba center in Boston.

Prior to an imaging test, Baba appeared in a dream: I'm in a crowded theatre, aisle seat; Baba walks in giving *darshan*, walking slowly towards the podium. He stops by me, takes my head, and gently puts his forehead to my forehead, twice. I wake up re-assured – Baba is on my case.

Live in the Present

We have been rehearsing a new song with the Bailey sisters, *Gratitude*, it tells Baba exactly what I am feeling with all my heart. In an interview, Baba said to me "Live in the present, live in the present, live in the present!" Even after an encounter with death, the monkey mind will continue with its antics. We walk around with a question mark on top of our heads, worrying about future events, muddling over past experiences. For this "walking miracle," Baba's easiest teaching is still his most profound: "Start the day with love, spend the day with love, end the day with love, that is the way to God."

185

OM SAI RAM

Song to Swami

We come with so much stress
To find a bit of peace
The trip is long and hard
But in the end is sweet.

Sri Sathya Sai, You are my friend
Sri Sathya Sai, You are my guide.

From New York to Puttaparthi
We come with high hopes for darshan
You give us Your love and blessing
We enter eternal bliss.

Sri Sathya Sai, You are my friend
Sri Sathya Sai, You are my guide.

Step by step we take towards you
To conquer doubting and sadness
Your guiding light is our hope, Lord
To walk in a fearless world.

Sri Sathya Sai, You are my friend
Sri Sathya Sai, You are my guide.

Vibhuti, amrith and bhajans
Your miracles leave us breathless
Perfection, wisdom and humor
Your wit is the perfect gift.

Sri Sathya Sai, You are my friend
Sri Sathya Sai, You are my guide.

Sri Sathya Sai

Glossary

Abhishekam	Ritual bathing of statue of deity
Akhanda Bhajan	A continuous 24 hour session of devotional singing
Amrith	Divine nectar
Ashram	Residence for saints and spiritual aspirants
Avatar	An incarnation of God
Ayurvedic	Traditional medicine of India
Bardo	Tibetan concept of transitional state between incarnations
Bhajan	Devotional song
Book of Brigu	Book of ancient Indian astrology
Darshan	Seeing a Holy person
Dasara	Traditional Indian festival of victory of light over darkness
Dervish Dance	A twirling dance of the Sufi Moslem tradition
Dosa	Pancake filled with potatoes or vegetables

Dhoti	Indian male garment wrapped around the waist
Durga	Female deity, embodiment of physical energy
Ganesh	Elephant-headed deity, remover of obstacles
Gayatri Mantra	Ancient Vedic prayer
Guru	Teacher, guide to spiritual liberation
Henna	Cosmetic adornment for hands, feet and hair
Homma	Fireplace used in Vedic rituals
Jnana	Wisdom, spiritual knowledge
Karma	Law of cause and effect in human actions
Leela	Divine playfulness
Lingam	An egg-shaped symbol of Shiva
Mandir	Temple
Mirabai	Indian female saint
Om	The sacred primordial sound of the universe
Omkar	Vedic chanting

190

Padnamaskar	Touching the feet of a Holy person
Prasad	Food blessed in devotional ritual
Prasanthi Nilayam	Abode of Peace, the ashram of Sri Sathya Sai Baba
Prema	Divine Love
Puja	Religious ritual, altar
Pundit	Religious scholar
Rakshasas	Mythological demons
Ramayana	An ancient Sanskrit epic on the life of Rama, a Divine incarnation
Sadhana	Spiritual discipline
Sadhu	Monk, renunciate
Sai	Sathya Sai Baba, divine mother
Samsara	The material illusory world
Saraswati	Goddess of wisdom and communication
Sathya	Truth, unchanging divine reality
Satsang	Gathering of like-minded spiritual aspirants

Satvic	Balanced, peaceful quality
Seva	Service
Seva Dal	Volunteers in the ashram
Shiva	God of the Hindu trinity (Brahma-creation, Vishnu-preservation, Shiva-dissolution)
Shivaratri	Indian festival to Shiva, auspicious time for self-realization
Swami	An affectionate name for one's spiritual teacher
Tamboura	Traditional drone string instrument, backdrop for Indian Classical music
Vedas	The most sacred scriptures of India, from ancient oral tradition
Veena	South Indian string instrument, associated with goddess Saraswati
Vibhuthi	Sacred ash, often materialized by Sai Baba, with healing properties
Yagna	Ancient Vedic ritual

Yoga	A path of spiritual discipline to reach God consciousness
Yogi	A practitioner of yoga

Made in the USA
Columbia, SC
04 October 2018